HPK1

IN THE STRONG WOODS

IN THE STRONG WOODS

A Season Alone in the North Country

Paul Lehmberg

St. Martin's Press
New York

Library of Congress Cataloging in Publication Data

Lehmberg, Paul.
   In the strong woods.

   1. Lehmberg, Paul. 2. Nym Lake region, Ont.—
Biography. 3. Nym Lake region, Ont.—Description and
travel. I. Title.
F1059.T5L43   971.3'12   79-25000
ISBN 0-312-41172-3

To Suzanne

Contents

strong—of country: thickly covered with
  undergrowth

—*Oxford English Dictionary*

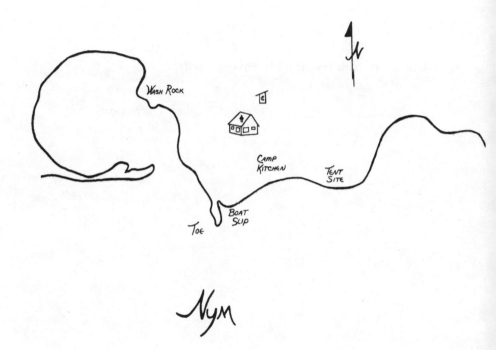

Wash Rock

Camp
Kitchen

Tent
Site

Boat
Slip

Toe

Nym

ON THE RIVER

Chapter One

Once it was my task to fan the dying coal of courage in the weak of heart. It was intense but interesting work—none of us did it for the money—and for me it was especially interesting on those afternoons I spent in the woods above First Rapids on the Kawishiwi River shepherding a variety of people through the various events of a ropes course at the Minnesota Outward Bound School. The ropes course was a fantasy land, a playground of marvelous heights and stretches, the stuff of dreams and ecstasies. But you had to be of a certain age—under twelve, say—to see it that way. It is in the early teenage years that the process of aging infects us with a certain conventional wisdom that convinces us to give up such dangerous foolishness as can be met with on a ropes course. For those who have surmounted their childish naiveté, perhaps by exchanging it for a manly prudence, this playground was not playful at all. Besides taxing physical capabilities, the ropes course probed and—so we hoped—strengthened the human heart. Which, of course, was the point of the whole thing.

1

I never lost my fascination for an event we called the flea's leap. It consisted of three stumps in a straight line that were about four feet apart and ten, six, and three feet high. The object of this whimsically titled event was, simply, to make your way in a series of jumps—or leaps—from the tallest to the shortest stump. Each stump had been topped with a sturdy, shingled four-by-four-foot platform to widen the base and improve traction. In case one of the human fleas should somehow miscalculate his leap, a thick bed of saw-chips lay below to cradle his fall—that is, if by some quirk he should break through the arms of the two spotters stationed on opposite sides of the leap.

What was it, I ask myself, that convinced my students to fly off the flea's leap to the platform below? They would stand at the outermost edge of the highest platform, knees bent a bit, eyes locked in fascination on the platform below them, and their arms would begin that hesitant search for just the right rhythmical swing to carry them out and away. But what was it that finally made them go?

I need to know, being perched on a flea's leap myself. Mine is of the imaginary variety, constructed not from sawed-off tree stumps but from what we loosely call mind, and though my flea's leap is by no means as solid as the real thing, it has turned out to be even more formidable. It is the sort of thing you don't notice yourself building until you recognize yourself up there high in the air, your tower finished. As I'm discovering, one flea's leap is pretty much like another: Up here it's the thought that counts; if you're here too long, it's the only thing that counts.

So I probe my memory of that flea's leap in the woods; I study it, to see how I might get myself down from my present mental height. Physically speaking, there wasn't much to that flea's leap above First Rapids, yet I saw in it a complexity, even a mystery, because more so than for any other event, it was hard—no, impossible—to say how difficult the obstacle was. It depended. But not on a sense of balance or on muscular strength. As I quickly discovered, average balance and merely minimal strength were aids enough to many a human flea trying to land safely on the stump below. The difficulty in the flea's leap depended almost entirely on what I at first judged to be a rather unimportant variable: whether you happened to be the leaper or an observer.

It was my job to convince the timid that they actually could cross this four-foot infinitude of space and land safely on the stump below. To that end I pleaded, praised, wheedled, teased, damned, dared, threatened, cajoled, lied, didn't lie—I even nudged a few—in order to imbue my charges with enough nerve or heart or faith, or whatever it was, to leap.

None of it, of course, did any good. I soon discovered that the successful leapers were those who never gave me a chance to pep-talk them into jumping. They—quite simply—jumped off the damn stump, and it was so plainly, so matter-of-factly done that the leap itself was not really very interesting to watch. What drama there was in the flea's leap—and there was usually little of it—preceded the jump itself. A few moments of—what?—and then into the air, and not so much as the slap of tennis-shoed feet against shingles to signal or symbolize the victory. These people would have jumped—and, somewhat to my disappointment, they did—without benefit of my earnest counsel.

On the topmost platform you quickly class yourself as either a thinker or a leaper. The leapers are nearly always gone inside of a minute, and those who stay past the minute become thinkers. The thinkers are discovering that the flea's leap is really a fool's leap, and so, of course, they seldom jump and sometimes have to be ignominiously brought down. What I had to say to both thinkers and leapers seemed to be heard not as good or bad advice or as right or wrong. I simply wasn't heard at all, as if I were static that had to be listened through instead of to. Public reasons and arguments do not seem to convince in a case like this. A reason, an argument, does not make you jump. What does? This is a private language, the private language of decision, and it is almost as if the leapers have been told some secret or have eavesdropped and caught a password or signal from somewhere. But no. It must be some kind of shock that makes you go, that arcs the void between the stumps, between the thought and the act.

The language of decision. I try to acquire fluency in it, enough fluency to convince myself to spend the coming summer, now only three months away, alone in the strong woods of northwestern Ontario. It is a hard, ice-blasted land of rock and water and pine, so thickly wooded that the lakes and rivers have always been the roads, whether for Indian, voyageur, lumberman, trapper, or miner. Now, by Provincial decree, the waterways are still the roads in this part of Ontario. Even though there is a world of water in this canoe country, it is like the desert: You can see the bones of the earth there. It is a somber country of elemental beauty that may at first be missed—or dismissed—but that is sturdy and lasting, like the bones themselves.

Five years ago my wife Suzanne and I, along with two other couples who are old friends, built a cabin there on the Canadian Shield, and even before the cabin was a blueprint I wanted to live there for a year or at least a season. Our cabin sits on the edge of a lake and can be reached only by boat or canoe, and our nearest neighbor is some miles away. As cabins go, ours is middle-sized, though still spare and simple. It was designed to be both lived in and looked at, and the windows are big, which is our one luxury, so that we are never too much inside. I think of the cabin as a wooden tent.

On the River

Though we have no name for our cabin, for convenience' sake I call it Nym, which is the name of the lake it borders. For Bob and Pam, Rick and Janet, and Suzanne and me, Nym was—but for a while only—a dream. We are romantics, but we were not incurable about it: Besides dreaming, we ferried the cabin board by board down the lake, toted everything up the hill, and sawed and hammered our dream into reality—and we were accompanied in the building not by the pipes of Pan but by the high bagpipe drone of mosquitoes. Now Nym is our base for exploring the canoe country along the Minnesota/Ontario border. It is a place to sleep long and to dream slow dreams that have an end. It is a place to separate the me from the not-me, to spend slothful and serious days skimming for silly thoughts and sounding for deep ones. At Nym you can do as you're of a mind to—watch the night sky for northern lights, read a book or make up a story, spit on a rock, saw and split wood, go berrying, bake bread and eat fresh walleye you have caught yourself.

Nym is a place to regain your senses and your sense. City life pummels the senses—we are forced into gluttony. There is too much to hear and see and smell in a city (to say nothing of the quality of what we hear and see and smell). On the corner where I live in Salt Lake City, the traffic never stops, and my senses are vandalized by the law—if it can be called that—of diminishing returns. I no longer hear the traffic—or rather, I hear it only between 3:00 and 5:00 A.M. on those mornings when the cars pass infrequently enough to be heard as individualized sounds. Perhaps I ought to be thankful that my body is resourceful enough to anesthetize me in this way, but I am not thankful. If we are living creatures, then we ought to be alive to our surroundings instead of dead to them. To be fully human means first of all to be an animal, and Nym is a place where our exhausted animal senses can restore their strength. A little craziness is a sign of life, and

Nym provides the chance to be again won over by the newness that sense discovers and to wander—if we are lucky—as crazy a trail as my dog Zip does. These are the first steps back to the equilibrium of sense.

We know that Nym is each of these things, yet there is much we do not know about Nym. Nym is not a home for us—it is too young to be that—but it is a homeplace, and the reality of the cabin has not destroyed the dream of it the way practice can do to a theory. Perhaps the reality and dream coexist because the dream of Nym is open-ended, even vague, in our minds—and that, I suspect, is the reason we have been unable to give a name to the cabin and our land. We like the thought that Nym as an idea or dream has almost a lifetime of growth left in it, and our uneasiness about naming is really our uneasiness about enclosing an idea and perhaps constricting or collapsing the dream. We have claimed the land and had it surveyed and been granted a patent to it by the Canadian Crown, and now the land slowly makes its claim upon us. Having tasted the fruit that can come of being bound to something, we want to explore and nurture that relationship, which is still in its infancy. We want to discover what it means and will mean to us individually and collectively, and as parents of children born and unborn.

And yet . . . somehow I cannot will myself to say yes to my wish—my dream—and feel good about it. Instead I find myself trapped atop this flea's leap of my own making, wondering not how to keep myself away from Nym, which would make some sense, but how to get myself there, which makes no sense at all.

Especially does it make no sense because at the age of twenty-eight, I have reached a juncture in my life. I am free. Nothing constrains me to stay here in Salt Lake City. Having just finished my preliminary exams (preliminary to what?), I

am now a dissertation removed from my Ph.D. in English.
But the exams so enervated me that I cannot bear the
prospect of a dissertation now—I haven t even enough
energy to choose a topic. Scholarly books, study carrels, the
stacks of freshman themes to read that have paid my way
through graduate school, all induce in me a faint—but
growing—narcolepsy. I am bored. And, after five years at it,
I am tired, tired of practicing the critic's craft of illuminating
literature—it is a ghostly life, your excuse for existence being
slight: that another writer has existed before you. But more
than this, I know that now it is my own life, and not the
literature I read, that needs illumination.

My marriage says so. Suzanne, my lovely wife whom I
cannot love, has moved out. Two months ago we divided up
the furniture and I helped her move into an apartment three
miles away. Left unwatched, our love escaped from us and
was replaced not with hatred or bitterness but with
nothing—a nothingness that weighs, like the noon heat of the
Utah deserts. The only feeling we share now is that *something happen*, and we look for signs from somewhere showing
us the way. But nothing happens. Mired in the stagnation of
our own doubts, we want more than anything to be charmed
by love, or even hate, for each other so that we can spring
ourselves out of this stop-time and get on with our lives.
Moving to Nym for the summer might give me the rest I
need; moving might quietly kill our marriage and give us the
corpse we need for burial; or moving might somehow bring
our marriage back to life.

Who can say?

II

It is April 15. A month ago there was no sure sign of spring
to believe in, but the tease of the past month seems over
now, replaced by promise. Wind, water, and earth look

7

committed to spring now, and the foothills about the city are powdered a dusty green. Down here in the valley every bud on every bush and tree is promising a leaf. With all the promises about, it was easier for me to promise something, and today I did. Today I bounded off my leap!

Curiously, it was quite easy. "Are you a man or a flea?" I demanded of myself. I wanted, of course, to be a flea—the leap is not so whimsically titled after all—and today I was a flea. I simply decided; I simply said it: "I will go to live at Nym," and then there was a moment of heartsink and some unaccountable hollowness, but they soon passed. I said the words aloud, low and to myself, because they were only for me. The words sounded strange and exciting, and in saying them it was as if I were somehow being magnetized by them. Saying the words aloud emphasized my resolve, and the words seemed more true for my having said them, just as in kneeling to pray, the religious act out and at the same time nurture their humility.

On June 8 I leave Salt Lake City to travel across 1500 miles of North America, my aim a cabin on a hill at lake's edge in the vastness of Ontario's canoe country. This date and my departure are thickly circled on the calendar hanging from my study wall. Today I won my heartsease.

III

This has been some spring. She got old fast. Agog from the shoots of green, spring's announcement that all things are possible—and right away—I leaped, but blindly, off my tower of indecision, only to discover that there was no platform below to cradle me. My heartsease soon left me, and it was the going public that drove her off. It happened like this, and it happened more than once:

I'm in a hallway, say, talking with a fellow graduate student I chance to meet. We are standing, in the middle of things,

8

taking some quick, nearly nourishing conversation the way we might grab a vending machine sandwich. She asks what my plans are for the summer. The question seems mundane enough, to her at least. But for me it is *déjà vu*. I had this conversation last week, and I scent a narrowing of the path and a trap set some few sentences off. I say something terse about going to Ontario for the summer, hoping she will change the subject.

It doesn't work. Instead of widening the path of our conversation, my vague answer further constricts it. Ontario is not a place she has ever given any thought. For her it is not a possibility, and she wants to know why it is for me. I mention I have a cabin there.

Oh, really? she says. Her voice ascends a few steps on *really*, and she clips the words, as if surprised into saying it fast. Her interest is up—this sounds charming—and our conversation is less casual now. A few more questions follow, and I answer them as guardedly as I can. Then I hear it, I see it, the trap being set: "But what will you do all summer?" I've just told her that except for a dog I'll be alone, and now the plan sounds more odd than charming to her. This is no longer casual conversation; this woman is really interested. She waits for me to put my foot in.

There is a break in the talk, nothing very noticeable, while I plan my strategy. I choke down my rising anxiety and at the same time try to decide what to do. Her patient but intent look tells me that she's really not interested in what I'll do—that question was merely polite. What she really wants to know is why anyone, when you get right down to it, would want to live alone for an entire summer in a cabin that is miles from the nearest road. She wants me to explain why my perversity is not really perverse.

What should I say? The fact that we're standing in a public corridor suggests that an answer of the twenty-five-words-or-

9

less variety would be suitable, even perfect. Perhaps she expects that someone with such designs as mine will have ready just this sort of answer to quickly satisfy any skeptics I encounter. But I don't have a ready answer. I could tell her that if she has to ask she'll never know—I believe that sometimes—but the answer is too cute, and I decide to save it for someone who is trying to bait me. Or maybe I should announce in a seriocomic vein that a summer in the woods offers the opportunity to achieve a life free of moving parts.

The lull in the conversation is a little more obvious now, but for her not uncomfortably so—yet, anyway. *Why?* The question flies back and forth in my head like a fishnet whipped again and again through its own hoop. Soon I'm thinking of myself thinking, which is no thought at all, only observation, and a vacuous one at that. I want to say, like a child, "Because."

In a matter of seconds some kind of disaster is going to happen unless I say something. Panicked by now, I decide that the only way I can extricate myself from this mess is to answer the question she really asked rather than the one she meant to ask. So I follow the letter rather than the spirit of her honest query. "What'll I do up there alone all summer?" I contemplate for her benefit. As I say these words a slight smile is forming on my lips, or at least one had better be forming. The smile, if it is there, is an accessory, as a tie is to a coat. I hope to appear slightly enigmatic, but not in an irritating way. Continuing to muse, I say half to myself and all for her: "Oh, I'll probably fish a lot."

I should have winked when I said it.

As I say, this happened more than once. My answers to the question varied a bit, and though they were not all as banal as this one, they all were in one way or another unsatisfactory. In this particular instance, though I failed in my attempt to appear winsomely enigmatic, I did manage—with some help—to make good my escape. My lame answer suggested to my kind inquisitor that she was being deviously invited to retreat from some very private property, and, supposing that she had begun to pry, she willingly—and deftly—changed the subject.

It was not the prying *per se* that so disheveled my well-being and dispirited me. I could have stood that easily, and I even doubt that I would have thought of it as prying had I been able to summon a more or less satisfactory answer—not so much for her as for myself. I had neither an answer of twenty-five words nor one of twenty-five pages. And I would have been glad for either.

In making public my commitment, I discovered where the hollowness had come from after I so ceremoniously announced to myself: "I will go to live at Nym." It was a premonition of where I was about to fly off to, caught up as I was in the madness of spring. I had sprung into a vacuum and I saw no platform below me after I leaped. My stiffly spoken promise was not a symbol of a decision but the decision itself, and symbol and object had wrongly become one. Winter, it turns out, is a better time to make a decision. You are more likely in those dormant days to make only those promises you ought to keep—and only those you can keep. I was thinking of reneging on my promise.

I am pragmatic—hard-headed—and, like Frederick Taylor, I like to be scientific about my hard-headedness. Taylor is an undeservedly obscure figure in the history of American culture. As the father of scientific management, he proved what many of us had long suspected, that bricklaying and pancake flipping were not really arts at all because there is always a good, better, and best method of accomplishing such tasks. Taylor taught us the best method, but more important, he taught us that this best method, if we could only discover

11

what it is, is best for everyone—no exceptions. Thus, Taylor is in that long line of Americans that extends from Benjamin Franklin through the modern-day practitioners of computerized cost/benefit analysis, which is the latest voodoo science of determining whether the game is worth the candle.

I am cast in that same American mold as Franklin and Taylor. Along with everyone else, I profess to be appalled by the dehumanization of the computer, but despite such lip service, I have found out how much I love, if not the computer, then at least the idea of it. I ask the question: Should I go to Nym? Then, based on dispassionate input, a lettered ball gyrating faster than my eye can catch it pecks out its block-letter recommendation, a bold YES or NO, onto the page. If the neatness is not enough and I demand to be dazzled, the machine can do that, too. Below the YES, it prints out in percentage points the margin of error in its answer. But what is most beguiling of all is that I would be instrumental in making this decision—that is, merely instrumental. I would be only a sourcebook, a feeder of information, and so escape having to make any decision at all.

To make my decision, I first needed a justification, even a philosophy, for going over the mountain to see what you can see. It was not enough to say vaguely that I wanted to explore the dream and the reality of Nym, or that I believe there is a certain rightness or naturalness, especially at this point in my life, in going to live at Nym for a season. Such feelings—they could be called nothing more than that—were too private, too brittle and fleeting. They were mere sentiment—desires, wishes, dreams, all of it nothing more than a kind of brain-fog. And, therefore, unbefitting the hard-headed. Act on sentiments like these and you play the fool.

So I hunted out reasonable reasons for going to Nym, and the search became an investment of sorts, like a mutual fund you pay into each month. Like any investor, I sought a return proportional to my investment—paydirt, justification. I needed the justification in order to go to Nym, but the longer I hunted for it, the more I needed the justification simply for itself. Having paid in my consideration these months, I deserved the justification for having the patience to throw good money after bad. It was, as they say, the principle of the thing. I had to know precisely what it was that I would gain by spending the summer at Nym. Did I, like Henry Thoreau at Walden Pond, want or expect to drive life into a corner and so discover its meanness or greatness? Or was I like Edward Abbey in the Canyonlands of southern Utah, in search of a "hard and brutal mysticism"? Or maybe, like Annie Dillard when she lived on Tinker Creek, I expected to be "carved along my length by unexpected lights and gashes from the very sky"? But before the fact, I could not even presume to such accomplishments as these without feeling detestably vain, even somewhat silly. But if not these things, what? Voices asked, Will the summer provide you with a *Weltanschauung?* Will it solve the dilemma of your marriage? Will it rest you enough to write a dissertation? If not that, will it increase your IQ ten points? five points, then? *What shall it profit you?*

Those were the things I had to know, and those were the things I never found out. It is late now, midnight. My duffle bag and two packs, a big box of books, and a smaller box, that one full of tools, rest against each other on the floor in the darkened living room. From my study I can see the gear silhouetted by the false moonlight shining through the window from the corner streetlight. Tomorrow morning I leave for Nym.

Tonight I am something else than packed: I am ready. Sometimes you need to be force-fed an idea, as I was these last two weeks by the silent run of time. Time kept passing, passing, and it threatened to run out before I could produce my justification for the future. Ground down by time, I retreated down a now-familiar path to ask—at last—the most elementary question of all: Is there any justification that is self-evident, one that needs no argument to give it validity? Of course there was. Nothing, as the saying is, succeeds like success, and the corollary to this truism is that success produces its own justification. The idea seemed so simple that it sounded vaguely stupid to say it.

Nevertheless, I decided to examine the idea. Justification, I decided, is the same thing as success except for one accident that distinguishes them: They are separated on a track called time. The separation between justification and success is the void between the thought and the fact accomplished, between the potential and the actual. My analyses, iterated and reiterated over the months; my constant considerations and reconsiderations; my accumulation of quasi-data for the informal cost/benefit analysis that I would run soon, very soon now; all the thought, all the talk-talk, could never justify because I refused to acknowledge the given: You can get there from here, but you have to leave here first. Unsure about what lay down that track, or even where that track went, I refused to follow it. When you are laid low by a fog, the sensible thing is to wait until it clears. But men are a combination of mind and matter who seek to marry thought with action, and you have got to let them ply one another.

How do you do it? I think it is best to become a bit blind. Scattered vision leads to scattered force, which in turn thwarts action and increases paralysis. The problem is to somehow blinder yourself like a horse in harness. It is all a matter of placing—or finding—yourself in the right position. For instance, in the position I by chance find myself in tonight.

On the River

I am anxious, expectant, in the same way I was when we shot First Rapids on the Kawishiwi River that spring at Outward Bound when the water was so high it reached up past the sand eddy and lapped the sauna door. In the slick swift water we picked our way, back-paddling at times, through the channel to the vee we had chosen. Just ahead of the chute there is a point, an instant unmistakable, when sternman and bowman simultaneously sense that here, right *here*, is the point of no return. From *here* on there is no choice. You will be irredeemably swept into the thunder and spume below. Then you are past that point in the vee— caught, committed, they come to the same thing. You are responsible, or perhaps irresponsible, only for reaching the point of no return. Once you are caught, the river will, or it will not, carry you the rest of the way, as your luck and skill dictate.

The trick is to get into the position, to let yourself get caught. I would think that that could knowingly be done. It was no trick with me—I didn't know I was being caught. Unaware, I snared myself on some words simply by saying them, and I think that must be how a lot of people catch themselves. A mere statement, and simultaneously the surprise, the shock, that it is my voice, me, saying it. Symbol and object are one and you have your rascally curiosity to blame. Watch out: You run the risk of becoming a true believer like Tertullian, who accepted Christ because he was so preposterous and because of the wonders to see if Christ were true. I was no Tertullian. My yea-saying lasted only moments until I was brought up breathless by the reckless-ness of my spoken words, fearful because they were—they are—electrifying.

I think of men who have been electrified, like Columbus, who set sail for what he supposed was Cathay. In the name of God and for Spain, Columbus sailed straight into the jaws of the unknown. Why? Those three traditional reasons, for

15

gold, glory, and God, could not have been enough. Those were the public reasons, the reasons of state. I think Columbus sailed toward the edge of the earth for the hell of it. Just to see. First there had to be the curiosity, the exciting bet with the self that there is something there worth seeing, never mind what it is. Other reasons, those public reasons that in part anticipate just what the trove is, come later.

The bet, impossible as it sounds, can sustain you. It can sustain because sometimes it is the only thing that remains. At least that is true in my case. I refused to act—to leap, to commit myself—because all reasons for living at Nym proved fickle. I could not tell in which—if any—of them success was intrinsic. Success had to inhere in the plan as oak-ness does in a planted acorn properly tended. But I was at last forced to give up such witchcraft, and my eye had all the while remained attracted by what I had always assumed was undependable, the curiosity, the bet with myself. Its virtue was its hardiness and strength. The bet was leathery and tough, always there. Such loyalty, I thought, deserved a like loyalty, and, nothing having come of my careful wisdom, I decided to cast my lot with foolery instead. All that wisdom had only worn me out. I will act on this bet and give myself the chance to play the fool. Something might come of it, this curiosity.

So. I am on the river and the vee is close. Wide-eyed, I am not at ease, exactly, but I am not ill at ease either. Something in between—anxious without the *angst*, maybe. Soon, very soon now, it will be too late. Maybe I ought not to be here. But the answer to that doubt lies in the calm waters below the rapids, or maybe directly in that tangle of rock and water. What I know is that I am at the vee. And that now is the time:

TRAVEL TIME

Chapter Two

Nym Lake lies on the southern edge of that great swath of coniferous forest that bands the earth in its higher latitudes. Botanists, safely combining at least this once the new with the old science, call this forest type boreal, after Boreas, Greek god of the north wind. To Eurasians it is the taiga. Canadians call it the bush, a name whose brevity and plainness suggest the anonymity that is inherent in its vastness. To me it is simply the Northwoods. I know only a chip of it, that area bounded by a line running from Duluth up the north shore of Lake Superior across Grand Portage to Thunder Bay, Ontario, from there eastward to Minnesota's water-bound Northwest Angle, and from that point back to Duluth 200 miles to the southeast. In the eastern half of this triangle is the land I know best of all, Ontario's Quetico Provincial Park, and bordering the Quetico, Minnesota's Boundary Waters Canoe Area (BWCA). Together the Quetico and the BWCA comprise over 17,000 square miles of wilderness area thick with forests of pine, spruce, aspen, and birch. Where there are no trees there is water—7000 square

17

miles of it—so much water that on a map the lakes and rivers give the appearance that they are odd strings and shards of turquoise that have been spilled in profusion from some great urn off in the far North.

Everywhere there are lakes, bogs, swamps, potholes, rivulets, streams, rivers. But mostly lakes, and Nym is one amongst the infinitude. It lies almost lost in this extravagance of water three miles above the Quetico and forty-five miles north of the international boundary. Nym's fantastic shape is spread amoebalike through the queer indentations in the earth's Precambrian crust, and its fingers and bays cover everything that is not at least 1350 feet above sea level. Those portions of the earth that have escaped the lap of water are littered with a thin and ragged mantle of soil and mosses, from which a second growth of reedy timber lives tentatively. Though the lake spans only six miles from east to west, its perimeter runs eighty miles and there are over 200 islands. Some of the islands are no more than rock outcroppings the size of a jail cell, and in their spareness—a stunted cedar, perhaps, or a white pine or two whose voluted shapes have been trained by constant exposure to the wash of wind—these tiny islands seem at turns whimsical or cruel, depending for their character on the sun and wind. Others, like Frenchy's island, are big enough to be easily mistaken for mainland if you do not have a map.

It is easy to get lost almost anywhere on Nym, easier here than on most of these lakes because of the fantastic profusion of islands. I myself have been lost here, I can't say how many times, my pride having prevented me from keeping a running tally of their number. During the blue August days that first summer when we ferried the lumber for the outhouse and cabin foundation that we built that year, I refused the aid of a map. Having guided canoe trips in this country for seven years, I knew some of the lakes—if perhaps not this particular lake—as I knew my own image in the mirror. And I was not unaware of the very unnaturalness of a man who needed a map to tell him where it was that he was building his cabin. That I could lose, literally lose my land, was an idea too ludicrous to admit. How could I make any claim other than a legal one to something I couldn't even find?

So, no map for me. I paid no heed that our too-shallow, too-short boat was most of the time precariously overloaded and that it threatened to dive downward with the speed but not the grace of a loon; I paid no heed to the fact that with only a three-horse outboard the round-trip sometimes took as long as two hours, depending on the load and the wind, and that we could not afford to waste time on unscheduled diversions around the far side of an island or up a dead end or into the wrong bay. I would prove my claim on the land by finding my own way into and out of the labyrinth of islands.

The claim proved suspect. Pride usurps its privileges and thus goeth before a fall—usually a number of them—and that was the summer I did my unscheduled—my secret—exploring. I gave myself lessons in putting the most charitable construction on an unfortunate situation. Finding myself lost, I would save the day by looking about with the intensest care, noting that this or that spot looked good for walleye, maybe, or that that one looked promising for bass, and then I would remark on the good fortune of my haphazardly won knowledge. I would be back, I thought, as I headed off in a new and more promising direction. The weather held for us that summer, and as it turned out my imperfect navigation never did upset our building schedule, and midway through the month I had the shortest route and all the reefs well memorized.

But now I know where I am. I know with some exactness. Where, precisely, is something that cannot be described with words, only with maps. A picture may or may not be worth a thousand words, but a map almost always is, and certainly here. For fun one day I plotted the coordinates of this .92 acre on maps of various scales that now hang tacked to the wall one behind another. A fishing map distributed by the Ontario Department of Lands and Forests describes Nym as lying 91° 26' west of the Greenwich Meridian and 48° 41' north of the Equator. But this information is offered only as an aside to fishermen interested in water depths who drive into the Nym roadhead, probably from the town of Atikokan, which is ten miles east of Nym on the King's Highway. The scale of the fishing map was too large to plot accurately the site of the cabin itself. So I moved to another map, this one of smaller scale, and determined that our land is bisected by 91° 26' 15" west and 48° 40' 45" north. But even that measurement was not very accurate. On a military map of even smaller scale I could be more precise. On this map, which Canadian Department of Defense cartographers have titled the Pickerel Lake Map in the Rainy River District of Ontario (by number: Ontario Provisional Map 52 B/11 in Edition 1 MCE of Series A 751), there is a metric grid system that has been superimposed on the primary grid of parallels and meridians by which we usually find our way about Earth. The cabin lies in the far northwest corner of this map in the square bounded by east-west metric grid lines 15 and 16, and north-south metric grid lines 92 and 93. This square can be further divided into hundredths to give an even more exact reading: Precisely, the cabin lies .2 square east of grid line 15, which gives an easting of 152; and .9 square north of grid line 92, which gives a northing of 929. The combined coordinate, then, is 152929. No matter your point of origin, and even were it dark, how could you with a map and compass fail to find me? (Though I have falsified the letter of my coordinate, the spirit of it is still true.)

152929. My amazement never ceases at the ease with which one can plot his physical position with such exactness. Having once lived on an Army base next to a place with the dreary name of Dairy Queen #4, I am not easily won over by numbers, and I claim as strong an irritation as anyone toward the numbers that year by year seem to increase their domination over us. Nevertheless, I admit to detecting something special in this number. It is my number, mine in a way that the Social Security number my government has tried to fit to me never can be. I like the rhythm of those six digits said in three-four time. My being charmed by a number probably has something to do with my acquisitive instinct, and, had I held the deed to Dairy Queen #4, perhaps I would have discovered a faint song in that number, too. 152929 is my only piece of property whose value does not annually plummet to a new low. I own it in legal partnership, the land having been granted by a letter of patent from the queen, Elizabeth II, Head of the Commonwealth, Defender of the Faith, for a sum we well and truly paid to her representative in the twenty-first year of her reign.

But more important than gratifying my acquisitive instinct—which is a rather base instinct anyway—the coordinates of the cabin provide me with a sense of comfort. One reason, of course, that I place special value on knowing where Here is in the cartographers' scheme of things is that for too long that first summer I was never exactly sure of where I was. It is always—simply—a good thing to know where you are, a fact that children, at least, never forget. The first act in achieving snugness in a limitless universe—I will assume for the moment that such an ideal can at least be approached—is to discover where in that universe you are, and in their own way the coordinates tell me absolutely where I am. Geologists would, of course, remind me of their scientific supposition that we are drifting northwest toward the Indian subcontinent at the rate of twenty feet a century, a theory that, if true, will render my coordinates meaningless. I accept their theory because it is their business to delve into such matters, and I am as fascinated—and unalarmed—by this piece of geologic trivia as I will be if I ever have the pleasure of reading a newspaper account describing the capture of a unicorn. They are right, 152929 is not absolute, but it is absolute enough. Measured in human time, it will hold.

Measured against the All my coordinate is a quasi-absolute, and at times I lodge an informal protest with myself that perhaps it should not provide as much primal security as it does. After all, a six-digit number on a map is not Truth—or truth, either, for that matter. It is instead a mere relation, the kind of scientific—in this case cartographic—"truth" that so disappointed Henry Adams. Perhaps, then, I should also be disappointed. The number is simply a formal introduction, something like the succinct definitions that anyone can look up in a desk dictionary. Such definitions are threadbare things that only limn a word and too seldom provide the nuances we need to really know it. So it is with my number. I do not intend to remain satisfied with it, and though the coordinate is not everything, it is something, and I would not deny that it has its satisfactions, no matter how elementary they may be.

So, by number and on a map I know where I am, but knowing has to do with something more than having plotted my whereabouts on a map: That I am well-oriented also stems from the fact that I took the time to arrive fully at these coordinates. Travelers don't always do that, especially those who span great gaps of time and space in airplanes. Jet travel is certainly our most efficient means of intraplanetary travel, yet that word *efficient* is in need of some important qualifications. Jets do a grand job transporting the flesh, less grand—especially for those who travel infrequently and to unknown places transporting the inhabitant of that flesh. I have discovered that it is risky to give over to a plane the responsibility for ferrying anything else than the body because that portion of me which lacks bodily substance falls easy prey to the disease we call jet lag.

Apparently there is some skill to flying that I have not acquired, perhaps because I fly so infrequently. Once I flew from Salt Lake City to San Diego for a wedding. I made our flight reservations some weeks in advance and then thought nothing about the trip until a few days before we were to leave. On the appointed day we drove to the airport, picked up our tickets—the appropriate cities and numbers had already been printed in a neat hand in the appropriate boxes—checked our bags, and boarded the plane. No hitches.

I could be accused, I suppose, of lacking travel sophistication—I am one of those people who must have a window seat—and, this being my first trip to California, I was much interested in tracking as closely as I could our approximate position during the flight to San Diego, which I knew in a vague way was a town somewhere south of Los Angeles close to the Mexican border. I got my window seat, but in only a few minutes after take-off we hit some "weather," as the stewardess called it, and there was no earth below to aid me in my amateur orienteering. All I saw was the *terra incognita* of thick cloud cover some thousands of feet below us. Soon everyone was presented with a tray of food, which I, at least, did not want, it being close to the middle of the afternoon. But, remembering that there is no such thing as a free lunch, I applied myself out of a sense of thrift, now grown somewhat spiteful, to awkwardly eating the unwanted meal in my cramped seat, and I gave up all thought of tracking our route.

For those presumably jaded travelers prone to boredom, the meal was timed perfectly. Just after the trays were collected, we landed amidst some anonymous urban sprawl. The intercom said it was Ontario, California. Into the air again ten minutes later, we were immediately offered another diversion, this time the soda pop of our choice. Before the stewardess had time to collect the plastic cups, we were in San Diego.

Ninety minutes it had taken us to fly from Salt Lake to San Diego! *Ninety minutes!* If I looked dazed as I walked down the ramp, and I must have, my face bore none of the ennui of the practiced traveler at the thought that he has survived the boredom of yet another flight: All I wanted to know was where I was. Even allowing for the 600 miles per hour that commercial jets are said to travel, how could we have come— to be excessively fair-minded—more than halfway? This place, if it was indeed San Diego, was too easily reached, but it must be San Diego even if there was fog, there were my in-laws walking toward us. Yet my certainty at being there was hardly unassailable; in fact, this wasn't certainty at all. This place had to be taken on faith, the kind Mark Twain talks about when you believe what you know ain't true.

The falsity of my physical position was obvious. For one thing, I had too little say—a mere phone call to an anonymous reservations clerk one month before—in choosing this place. Further, there was nothing I could detect in our circumstances that looked remotely potent enough to have worked our displacement of nearly 800 miles in the span of one bland meal. If I had indeed flown that far, why wasn't I in Omaha or Phoenix instead? Only, it seemed, because the words *San Diego* had been penned onto the tickets by someone. But that wasn't a reason, it was a fortuitous coincidence, an excuse deviously dressed out as a reason. I might have eaten the same meal and drunk the same cup of

24

pop and landed in Denver instead—in fact, I have. Being in San Diego didn't compute, except mathematically. Better to have walked here, I thought, two steps forward and one step backward like the pilgrims of the Middle Ages, or to have thrown my rented suit into the back of a Mormon handcart and pulled that across the deserts. Vapor trails through the clouds serve poorly as connective tissue, and the track of my steps would have forged a believable chain back to my point of departure. As it was, this place seemed connected to nothing. Had I walked, my burning feet and bone-weariness would have convinced me that there was some substantiality to this place. The trouble is that I would have missed the wedding.

I failed to arrive in one piece, as it were, and, as might be expected, the means of arrival colored the being there. First we were driven to a motel where reservations had been made for us. It was one of those motels whose self-advertised claim is that if you are loyal to its brand name, the room you will sleep in tonight is exactly like the one you slept in last night—or at the worst, a mirror image of it. Such an appeal may prove enticing, maybe even irresistible, to a small number of salesmen who must travel constantly, but it added nothing to my sense of the city's character or even of where that city was. I wanted a room with 800 miles of difference to it.

During the weekend, in order that everyone might be in the right place at the proper time, we out-of-towners were placed in the protective custody of a native San Diegan privy to the secrets of travel on southern California freeways. With Prussian efficiency we were rushed back and forth to the bride's parents' house, our motel, the church, the site of the groom's dinner, and various restaurants and bars, all places that dotted the cityscape with the randomness of dice dropped on a board. Thinking after a while that I knew something of the layout of the city, I would attempt what I thought was a reasonable, if not entirely educated, guess as to how long it would take us to reach the next checkpoint in what was becoming a weekend road rally, and if I felt particularly confident, I would even hazard a guess as to our route. But each time we got into the cars, there was a shake of the dice. I was lost the whole weekend.

I slipped back into Salt Lake that Sunday night with comparative ease, due no doubt to the fact that I had never managed to convince my cantankerous chief inhabitant to get off the plane once it had touched down in San Diego. With the aid of a road atlas I tried that night to retrieve myself retroactively from the void where I had just been, and though I determined as closely as possible where San Diego was in relation to Los Angeles, Ontario, and other cities, and though I carefully noted the names and positions of outlying suburbs whose names I had heard spoken so knowingly only hours before, it was impossible to establish a sense of the place after being there. My experience plainly attested to the fact that this place had no sense, no physical relationship to anything else. Maps by definition provide us with relationships, and I could not superimpose my experience onto a city that now appeared only as a name on the southern end of a dog-leg state bordering the Pacific. Believable events happen in solid places, and because San Diego was unmoored and immaterial, it seemed only a minor breach of common sense to then suppose, as I found myself doing, that I had gone to the reception before the wedding or the rehearsal.

Jet travel is sufficient for traveling salesmen and members of wedding parties—after all, the chief purpose of such a trip (your wishes aside) is not to know where you are. Supersonic speeds can be borne by such people, but they are a burden on those who crave the luxury of discovering the texture of a place. To feel this takes time, both in the preparation and in the act itself.

Travel Time

Time, or its passage, is the minimum preparation. Not only people but places can become tarnished through too-close association. A friend of mine tells me that, ocean travel being a bore and good for only a sunset or two, he decided to fly to Europe for his six-week vacation. Why waste time in a deck chair when you can add another country or two to your itinerary? After almost instantaneously breaching the gap between the New and the Old Worlds, he landed in London, and during the two weeks he had allotted for England, my friend found himself victim at unpredictable moments to the unsettling heresy that the entire country had been done up in the English motif by some Disneyesque entrepreneur with an obviously practiced eye for detail. No matter that he recognized the illusion for what it was. Illusion is like pain, never a phantom, and mere recognition of its existence is not the act of will that effects its disappearance. His quixotic illusions subsided, he says, about the time he would have docked in London, and England, the country he wanted most to visit, no longer holds any charms. It is the only country that can be collapsed like a circus for moving to the next town. Take a boat! he counsels now, and get there when you get there.

I am not the only jet laggard, and my own experience reinforced by another's convinced me not to waste my time trying to fly to Nym—I could have flown as far as Thunder Bay, which is 120 miles east of Nym. Instead I made the trip in legs, stopped along the way, talked with friends and fellow travelers, and in all took a week in the coming. By car and train and boat I came, making slow intentional time, the kind of good time I never made on a plane. In choosing my own routes, in choosing when to stop and when to travel, I was being as responsible as I knew how. There is nothing arbitrary about being in precisely this place. It is a place connected by paths of my choice to each place and event of the last week, but in its stark simplicity it is unlike everything of the past week—or the past year since I was here last—and thus is not connected too closely. Nym is new and different, apart from all else, too, and I find it a convincing place, coarse-grained and too palpable for loading onto a flat-bed. The inner impression is precisely aligned with the outer reality, and I feel under no self-conflicting obligation to make Twain's leap of bad faith.

The cars, trains, and boat brought part of me to Nym; what happened in them brought the rest of me. My chief resident is not easily sustained on a bland meal served at 35,000 feet. It takes something more by way of experience. This time it took, for one thing, cursing a Siamese cat named Mona during an all-day ride hitched with a friend from Salt Lake to Billings, where I would catch the train. No lover of cats in general, and allergic to this one in particular, I swore at the cat in silence—out of respect for its owner—and wondered at the fury with which cat hair could make eyes itch.

A college girl also played her part in my being here. She would be surprised and perhaps regret her assistance. My first evening on the train, the dining-car waiter seated her opposite me at the table, which was spread with stiff white linen and set with silver. Separating us was a solitary yellow rose nodding from a cut-glass vase, and our table was cast in the evanescent amber of the setting sun. We should have been in love. But I settled for a few questions, hoping for an agreeable dinner. She was, she answered, a college freshman traveling home to Illinois for the summer. Unbidden, I said that I taught freshman English, though not at her school. For the remainder of the meal she would say nothing, and her crusty silence I understood as a shorthand expression of her convictions, which I guessed were recently won, about that subclass of teachers to which I had admitted to belonging. It needed no saying that she had done with theme writing for a lifetime.

Others are responsible for my trip, too, one Sheldon Salzman, self-described opera composer; and a porter really a chamber musician momentarily defeated in performing for a living his works of love. With the wheels click-clacking in satisfying rhythm and the domed bar car swaying between the lengths of rail, we talked far into the night across the flats of North Dakota about many things, but mostly about what I cannot fathom, of how it is that a man can hear music in his head that no one has ever heard before.

A couple in late middle age played their part. Driving north from Minneapolis in a borrowed car, I stopped to eat somewhere north of Hinckley where you are through the corn and soybean country and the air begins to cool a bit and smell of northern pine. At the window of a white aluminum-sided trailer in a graveled lot, I ordered a chicken dinner from the woman, and after her husband prepared it, she tapped on the sliding window and smiled to signal that it was ready. I wondered how she could smile, living her life serving chicken from a trailer window, but then I opened the plain white box, the same kind that prom corsages come in, and tasted the chicken, and I knew why she had smiled. She and her husband had a secret recipe that was worth its secrecy.

And so it was. Unlike my meal eaten above the clouds, which passed the time, these people filled my time. I am a debtor they know nothing of: They interceded for me on behalf of myself by providing 1500 miles of life for the same distance traveled. Instead of anesthetizing me as a plane does, they enlivened me. Because of them something happened, and I am made believable in my own eyes. Remembered experience is in its own way a kind of substance, earthy and offering proof to the mind. Experience can be an argument—which most of the time is uncomplicatedly implicit unless some necessity forces it to explicitness—for a position assumed, and what I can safely assume and do assume, and what is not in need of some crazy proof, is that I am here. This time, all of me together.

The seventh evening I crossed the lake through a languid gray mist that seemed asleep on the water, and then I slipped the prow into the vee of peeled aspen logs that cradles the boat in the lee of a jutting rock I call the Toe. Back in the small clearing next to the landing, a fresh layer of pine needles covered the damp ground, and some trees had been ripped up by their roots from winter storms, but everything else seemed the same as when I had left a year ago. Looking up the hill through the straight jackpine, I traced the outline of the dark-stained cabin walls and the steep pitch of its roof shingled in forest green. It looked not to have aged at all, and if that were so I wondered how long it was that I had been gone. I walked up the hill and went through the rite of return, lifting the window shutters from their hooks and stowing them under the cabin, fetching the key to unlock the door, and sweeping the wood floor of what little dirt had accumulated over the winter. In an hour I had all my gear up the hill and stored in the spare sleeping alcove that is my pantry and storage, and I had moved in.

Tired that night, I sat at the kitchen table and followed the fantastic shapes of giant shadows cast onto the walls by the solitary flame from the table lamp. Then I noticed a change which I wait for but that never fails to surprise: The cataract of sound that ceaselessly thrums through my ears was beginning to subside. Beneath me I could detect the life-breath pulsing through Zip's nostrils as she dozed underneath me curled in amongst the chair legs, and hearing her slow breath was the exception which reminded me that here the welcome rule is silence. The quiet was a perfect expression to end the journey, like those seconds of enthralled silence before the mad applause of thankfulness for a great symphony greatly performed.

But to a journal keeper silence is never golden for long, and I thought to freeze this moment like an object in a photograph. Struggling out from under a wave of sweet exhaustion, I decided to write something. Uncapping my pen, I wrote of an end and a beginning. "I am here," I scratched onto the blank golden page—and knew only after I had written the words that they were the applause which always stands in the shadow of the silence. Nevertheless, I liked the words for their one virtue, which was their plain and solid manner, and so wrote them twice more to see if by repetition I could add anything to them. "I am here, I am here," I printed carefully again, "in the land of water." And then, after the words had dried to some permanence, I capped the pen and blew out the lamp.

WOLFING

Chapter Three

Here some old saws need reworking—it's May, not March, that roars in like a lion and retreats like a lamb. Each May, torn and ragged winter clouds scud low over the North, and winter snow and spring sun contend with each other like cobra and mongoose. In both rituals the contest is never in doubt, and by the first days of June the weather is noticeably tamer. But spring must have arrived earlier than usual this year. I had really hoped for more bluster in the air, and I wanted to shiver at sundown, to be placed under the necessity—it's such a comfortable necessity—of having to fire up the Franklin stove to burn off the evening chill. But the days and even the nights have been warm, and what signs are left of spring's flurry are quickly fading and almost gone.

Brushing the path that winds from the cabin to the Toe is a four-foot balsam fir over which I've kept unofficial watch since the day we cleared the trail and decided to grant the tree a reprieve against the saw. Each spring it shows off a chartreuse fringe of new growth, and now the brilliantine of the new needles is fast darkening to a tougher green. Ferns

33

have unrolled their fiddleheads and are now too tough for good eating. The aspen, birch, and moose maple are all fully leaved, and over to the east of the cabin early summer flowers are blooming. In a sparse stand of jackpine, pink lady slippers—orchids of the North—are scattered in ones and twos across a thick sponge of moss. But the most convincing sign of summer is that in the span of a mere two weeks, baths have become less memorable experiences. They are no longer the stuff of a tall tale. The bathtub—the lake, of course—is never a place where one tarries for long, except during the August dog days of the hottest summers, but now the lake no longer feels as if it were freshly filled with glacial melt-water. The ice, even any suspicion of ice, has melted and summer is here.

No one has been at the cabin since last February when Rick and Jan, towing a toboggan loaded down with three-year-old Jon, skied in across the ice to spend a few days. Unused to any human activity for so long, the cabin and even the woods close by seemed stiff, like a wet boot left too long to dry on the stove fender. The place needed breaking in again.

Or so, at least, was my first thought. It was a pathetic fallacy that in two days was laid bare by my own bone and muscle. Within forty-eight hours after arriving, my legs and arms and back—even my stomach—had tightened like drying leather into sore knots. It was I who needed the breaking in. My bones brittled and I ached to sleep off this preternatural tiredness that had descended on me, from where I could not tell. Stiff, I slept more than my customary eight hours, ten hours one night, then eleven, then twelve, but despite the sleep, which was as deep as my exhaustion, I woke each morning cotton-brained and lame and spent half the day fighting off etherization. Then, after the sixth of these hibernetic sleeps, the malaise broke like a fever, and I woke

Wolfing

before the sun had pinked the eastern horizon feeling fine-
tuned and lithe and as healthy as I had ever felt. With a
suddenness that was nothing if not strange, my body was
once again willing to work in my service.

Perhaps my temporary enervation was a growing pain in
sympathy with the new summer season. Perhaps. More
likely, though, it was irritability and rebellion registered by
certain sets of muscles forced into a new specialty, that of
daily fetching water from the lake in two five-gallon plastic
jerry cans. Though this chore does require a burst of
energy—especially up the short but steep rock face that
slopes to where I draw my water—it is still only a burst, the
entire span between the lake and cabin covering not much
more than a hundred yards. The cause of my inertia therefore
didn't seem solely attributable to the brute task of hauling
water. My pains had to be in part psychosomatic. If they
were the physical result of the switch from city to woods life,
they were also, I decided, a sign induced by mind to tell me
that I am in a new place to which various adjustments must
be made. It happens that you can't move into a cabin in only
forty-five minutes.

The adjustment, this refitting myself, took some days, and
it was largely a matter of reacquaintance, which would not
have been necessary at all were memory not so vexing. We
usually depend on it the way the middle-aged athlete does
his trick knee, which is to say that our faith in each is as
implicit as it is indiscriminate. Better to depend on the trick
knee—at least its failings are immediately obvious.

Take my trick memory. This last winter I could recall at
will and with great fidelity—I can verify this because the
object in question is not twenty feet out my window, and I
can study it at my leisure—the young balsam that is finished
in chartreuse. I remembered its queer diamond shape, the
dusty dull green of its flat needles, and the sheen on the new

bright needles after a rain. In comparing my image of the tree with the tree itself, I uncovered no incongruities, and in a way it was a surprise to discover no surprises at all. Memory's image had not been dulled or generalized by time, and if memory could summon particular trees, it could also command their combination, that entity called the woods. Memory rushed in to perform the task of creating an image of the forest that is my environment now, and the product which resulted from multiplying the sights and sounds was for a long time convincing, but after a while I thought I detected that the image before me was too stylized, too pale, too generalized, too . . . something, I couldn't—still can't—tell what. The combination of the trees is an abstraction of a higher power, and, inundated by the complexity of it all, I discovered that memory was overextended. I had lost the forest. Even, it is true, most of the trees.

Had I a mere affection for Nym, it is possible that I would never have recognized my too-solid faith in the powers of memory. And had I recognized it, I might have contented myself with the loss, rationalizing that this distortion or fading was a minor matter. But I am an *aficionado*. Where Nym is concerned, I demand much of memory, too much, as is common with *aficionados*. We are not nostalgia-ridden, and ultimately we care nothing for memory. Our passion is for the thing-itself, and we require perfection of memory in our assumption—our hope—that if, when we are separated from the object of our passion, memory is perfect, then image and object can be made one. Intemperately requiring perfection, we meet with failure instead, a failure that is bittersweet: bitter, because any loss of memory insinuates that your *afición* is more weak than strong—that it is not *afición* at all, and that the sum total of you is as false as your memory; but sweet, too, because forgetfulness allows one to return in order to purge memory of its falsehoods and then to reexperience anew the thing-itself.

Wolfing

Drawn by the sweetness, I spent portions of my first days
walking about by through my patch of woods sloughing off my
stillness, correcting those parts of memory that had lost
authenticity and redrawing what the rub of time had erased
over the winter. If there was no path to follow, and there are
few of them here, I meandered through the woods or along
the shore, marking as I went both the ordinary and the
extraordinary: a snapper the color of baked mud sunning
himself on a rock near shore; a dead pine three feet thick at
the butt split to the heart by lightning; slabs of cool heavy
greenstone; a tuneful unseen bird hidden away high at
treetop; the stony deep furrows of white pine bark; these and
more. If I knew that I knew them, I tried to recall common
names from out of memory. At familiar spots I stopped and
spent some quiet time, maybe only minutes, maybe an hour
or more, stretching my five senses that had grown dull under
city assault, regathering the minutiae of favorite or fre-
quented spots.

One of my favorite spots is right out the southeast bay
window between the cabin and the lake, and the path to the
Toe where the boat is moored borders its northwest corner.
It is our old camp kitchen. The spot sits twenty feet above the
lake, and the height offers a fine view of the lake and the
pine-dark southern shore in the distance. The kitchen is
spread mostly with jackpine, and there are some aspen, a few
birch, and a white pine or two. Before we began building,
the camp kitchen was indistinguishable, at least in a general
way, from any number of lookouts on this northern shore.
The forest floor was thick with foliage—moose maple, birch
and aspen shoots, and other small plants and shrubs, each of
them struggling for a place in, or out of, the sun. Because of
the fine view and the exposure to the breeze, which would
relieve us of at least some of the bugs, we built our fireplace
there and strung the dining fly over the newly constructed
picnic table, and it was there that we ate our meals and each

night talked over the next day's building as we sat around the fire. More than the brush hook, it was simply the tramp of builders' feet that cleared the spot of everything but the trees themselves, and now it is open and parklike, the ground luxurious with pine needles and woodchips.

The hallmarks of the camp kitchen's new civility are two rough chairs fashioned from peeled aspen saplings that we brushed coffee-brown with some wood stain left over from the cabin. Winter and summer the two chairs preside there next to each other facing the lake, and despite their spareness, which is so unrelieved the chairs look unfinished without someone sitting in them, they are comfortable. I have sat in the bigger one for hours at a time, and one windswept afternoon, book in hand, I decided to try it out again. Curling around a few nonfunctional protrusions and oddities in the aspen frame, I searched out a comfortable position, cracked the spine of a fresh paperback, and turned to page one.

Crude chair or not, the spot was too rich to begin a new book. There were too many diversions, and my attention flitted about like a butterfly. I felt like a boy at the circus wishing there was one less ring so he could be sure to see it all. I was diverted first by the harridan rasp and screech of a chipmunk grown murderous over my presence—or, more likely, Zip's presence—and then I was sidetracked from the harangue above me by the rheumatic groans of a jackpine whose limbs were being teased by the gusting wind. Off the edge of the page I could see flares glancing off the waves out on the lake, each shot of light as bright against the blue waves as a match sputtering alive in the dark. And on page ten, wondering what I had read, decided to give up. Since I could reserve the book but nothing else, I closed its covers and turned loose my attention and followed it.

As familiar as our open-air kitchen is the spot where

Wolfing

Suzannne and I spent our nights in the big umbrella tent until the cabin was habitable. The tent site is a hundred yards up the shore to the east of the old kitchen atop a huge granite knuckle that slopes steeply to a tiny bay. The edges of the knuckle are bedded with jackpine, and its center is strewn with stiff tufts of reindeer moss that always remind me of reef coral. We chose the spot because it offered a near-flat tent site, and because here at dawn we could look east down through the canyon of pines and wait for the first edge of light to break across the bay.

I was there my first morning to wait for the sun. My blood still thick from sleep, I walked back and forth to quicken it and to ward off the shivers until the sun could take over. The tent site did not look as ragged and matted this year, the scars from our sleeping bodies having faded a bit more, and I was pleased to see its more natural state. I picked my way through the moss down the rock knuckle to the water's edge and hung my towel on a familiar pine bough. Tracing the frozen boundary between lake and shore, my eye caught on a rock which in past years had performed blamelessly in keeping our toothbrush cases from rolling off into the lake— and I remembered that I had forgotten my toothbrush at the cabin. Bending deep at the knees, I cupped water and threw a shock of it to my face, then toweled dry and sat on a rock to wait in the stillness.

There it was!—out of a cloud-free sky lightened to a cream yellow by its own coming, the first direct light broke off the upper rim of the sun and angled toward me, picking up speed as it came my way. It struck: The day was born and I had been witness. Not that it was in need of witnessing or required a recording secretary. I was only a supernumerary—a mere hanger-on—but glad to be there again in any capacity.

When we slept on that rocky rise it was my habit, perhaps

39

my ritual, to wait like this for first light. There is a special vigor to dawn light that is brash but most forgivable, and things seen in this light appeal to my imagination because they are faceless and have shouldered none of the craggy and set character cast by dusk light. Simply, all things look possible because all things look new. Then, as it usually does when everything speaks newness, thought blighted the moment and threatened to destroy it even sooner than time will. Nothing gold can stay, least of all the dawn, and I watched time move, quarter-sun, then half-, then full-, and the day visibly aged as the sun moved above the tree line and back into its traces. The light cast by the full sun looked more flat than pure, and certainly not as interesting, and already it had lost some of its tone, like an aging muscle. In this older light fewer things seemed possible, and for a moment or two I regretted that such poignant freshness is no more likely to be trapped than is wildness.

But I drew back from the edge of melancholy, saved by the knowledge that on every clear morning the ineluctable newness predictably waits. Such easy predictability amounts to a standing dare to be there, if not to capture the freshness, then at least to begin the day in the company of beauty. Though the morning freshness had proved as nimble as ever, there was tomorrow and tomorrow, and as I walked back to the cabin warmed but hungry for breakfast, I knew I would be back for more dawns.

But not very often, at least not yet, my recent enervation having resulted in my sleeping straight through the best of the morning beauty. Such absence is a secular sin and I pledge to reform. But missing the sun is, besides a sin of omission, a privation. I like beginnings and endings and feel some small compulsion to be there to see things complete, but thus far I have been faithful only to the sunset. Sometimes I sit on the cabin step and watch the sun sink down slowly into the trees, their trunks thickly edged with a fiery molten gold that darkens to a loss energetic orange as night comes on. But I like best the unobstructed view because of the surprises it offers, so most evenings I walk out onto the Toe, and because the close sweep of trees to the north and west blanks the view in those directions, I scan the south and east skies that net the reflections of the lowering sun. I am at the Toe to be dazzled by the infinitely varied play of cloud and light, and though I cannot claim always to be dazzled, I have not yet been disappointed, and often I am amazed.

The Toe is a rock of some importance. There is nothing impressive about its appearance, no swirls or veins of contrasting texture or color to lend it distinction, no exotic shapes to single it out from memory. It is granite, but being the color of old chewing gum, it is not the stuff from which monuments are chiseled, and it protrudes from shore for twenty feet or so before it sinks out of sight to the lake floor. In shape it actually resembles a finger more than a toe, but I chose the latter designation because it is more in keeping with the predominant impression left by this jutting, pock-marked rock. It is grotesque, like a toe almost always is, no matter how shapely the leg, and like a finger almost never is. Grotesque, yes, but like your big toe, important: If you come here, you come by boat or canoe, and the Toe, quite simply, is the most obvious place to land because it looks to be the only place to land. So you point the prow along its eastern edge and tie up to the closest tree, which happens to be a paper birch. No matter from what quarter the wind, the east-ern edge of the Toe provides a well-protected slip despite the expanse of open water to the southeast, and a boat—for some reason—can ride out almost any storm without having to be hauled up into the clearing. Whether I have been gone for an hour or a year, the Toe is the first thing I see when I arrive, the last when I leave; its presence is undeniable, impossible to overlook.

It is hard to love a rock, but familiarity in this case has bred something more palatable than contempt, and I admit to a certain liking—affection—for this one. The Toe will never wear out; it serves well, and not only as a boat slip, dock, and site from which to scan the evening skies. From reading the cabin log that we keep, I know that more than one liar casting his line from the Toe's end has done battle with twenty-pound northern pike. My fishing rod leans handily against a near tree ready for a few casts from the Toe in the mornings and evenings, and though my luck has not yet been spectacular, I harbor hope and patience, and I do sometimes catch a meal's worth, which is the truth. The Toe is also my diving board, providing quick entry to—but not quite quick enough exit from—a brisk bath. In this nearly sandless country it is my beach, and after a midday dip, I drip-dry there when the sun is out and the wind warm, and despite its tortured surface, I sometimes doze there under the illusion that I am lord of the natural realm, at least that part of it within sight. By night from the Toe I watch the moon and stars, and by day squinting through binoculars I spy infrequent canoeists and fishermen who pass by on the far shore on their way east to the end of the lake to fish or to reach the racers' portages that lead south out of Nym from Black Bay into Pickerel Lake and the Quetico.

From the Toe I keep watch as from a window to see how it is with the world. Several times each day, some days almost every hour, I walk down to the Toe's edge, and sometimes I have not known exactly what it was that brought me there. Just the same, I stand there for a few minutes, or perhaps sit down and rest my forearms loosely across my indrawn knees, and note what particulars have changed in the design of things since I was there last. The particular might be the sign of a canoe party, the far-off sun-flash of a wet paddle worked through the water and then on the upstroke feathered to catch the least wind. Or, as a few days ago, it might be the tender murmur of thunder, so indistinct it could have been imagined. While my ears searched out the sound the way eyes might a coin lost in well water, a savage beat of wind rushed at me from nowhere threatening attack, and my stomach fell like a trapdoor and my blood fired. Whatever it was, it had swept low down the shore and passed behind me at strafing speed, its wings pumping mechanically as if they ran on gasoline, and in their relentless beat they seemed to overpower rather than finesse the air. Only after it was past did I get a look at the cause of such infernal noise. Banking against the shore and wheeling toward open water was the root of my witlessness, a solitary loon.

And that was how it was those first days. My muscles belligerent and my joints cranky and in need of some magical *aqua vitae*, I walked about to wear away the tightness. I paid calls to a couple other places, too, like the bower tree. It is a giant white pine behind a hump of rock back in the woods, where on windy days I used to escape the thrash of wind to read in the stillness beneath its branches. I also visited the Wash Rock, which is a flat expanse of exposed bedrock that borders a tiny lagoon which extends to the north just behind the Toe. There I do my wash, and after sunset I walk down there to watch the fanciful flights of bats skirring through the blue dusk. The Wash Rock is also my workshop—my canoe, a worn but venerable seventeen-foot Seliga, is sitting down there now on two sawhorses, her last coat of paint drying in the sun. After I had visited all the familiar spots, I went back. Then I went back again. In a general way everything looked much as it did last year, which is how I wanted everything to look, and I was never startled by any of the particulars it had become my occupation to discover. Except by that crazed bird.

It proved instructive to have my hair raised by a loon. Thinking about it later, I wondered how it could happen that the harmless flight of a loon could father such primitive if fleeting terror. True, there was the element of surprise, but that could not account for all my fright. After all, loons and I had surprised each other like this before, and in the same spot. More than once I have heard the stage-whisper whir of strong wings above me. There is no sound quite like it, and to those who have heard it, the sound is unmistakable. Unmistakable? Then why did my adrenalin falsely pump forth, armoring me for a fight to the death?

If you ask the right question, it can unloose a secret jam of thoughts. Though the answer to this one was simple, it turned out, nevertheless, to be a kingpin question. Plainly, the loon had so frightened me because it had been at least a year since I had last heard the eerie beat of strong wings at such close quarters. I had simply forgotten the sound. The unique rhythmic beat of those wings was like a word that I had at one time used often because I found some special value in it, but that now lay dormant in nether-consciousness, abandoned to that lesser category of words which I know only passively if at all. Abandoned: such a black word, but one that rose to thought as naturally as a bubble in water. The word suggested itself, and it was the internal particular that sparked the question of my present relationship to Nym. Surely there was something strange, or at least hidden, in these repeated excursions to all my favorite spots?

It was more than nostalgic indulgence, I decided, more than the lazy pleasure of the dilettante sauntering about gathering particulars that are interesting or amusing for their own sake. There was too much method, too much compulsion—though well enough hidden from me—in my sauntering. I had a secret purpose, I was not simply wandering about aimlessly. No, I was making rounds, walking a route as a milkman does Or a wolf. It occurred to me that these walks made my presence here obvious and pervasive in a very short time, and that through them I was attempting to reappropriate what I had abandoned over the winter. I was wolfing. A wolf will claim territory by ranging through it and directing a shot of urine at what he considers strategically placed trees, and I was indulging in the same primordial act, except that I constantly aborted mine. As a member of the most intelligent species of animal, I am endowed not only with the imagination that can create a symbol but also with an accompanying sophistication that allows me to appreciate my creation; thus, I was content with the symbol of ownership, the walks alone, and I felt no need to leave my sign, my smell.

But a wolf, spared the knowledge of his own consciousness, passes water to convince others, not himself. For me to convince others, the Crown has provided me with a letter of patent that includes my name, but I have an additional need, and that is to convince myself that my usurpation is proper, and this collection of idle facts that I was gathering on these methodical meanderings was covertly utilitarian. For men, knowledge of a place is the first acceptable claim of ownership, and I was engaged in amassing a working knowledge— knowledge that would work to reclaim what I had abandoned through my year's absence.

At first I was startled by the loon looking for a runway on the water, then troubled by it because it reminded me of other items less graphic that existed barely alive in the dregs of memory. I had even forgotten sounds I had heard hundreds if not thousands of times before. How was it that I could have been surprised in again hearing the ragged *THWACK-ack!* of the cabin screen door flapping loosely shut in its frame, or by the open-ended *hu—!* of the outhouse door as it whispers shut, reminding me, just as it probably did the last time I heard it, of a shotgun heard from far, far off? I had not heard these sounds for a year; perhaps I had not even thought of them in a year, whence my surprise and delight—at first—in hearing them again. They are innocuous sounds, it is true, but they are as characteristic of Nym as any, and to have let them slip unnoticed from memory would be nothing, except that I claim to be an *aficionado*, a devotée, a lover. But does a lover forget the sound of his loved one's laughter?

Through the window I can hear the flinty clatter of aspen leaves spangling in the afternoon breeze. It is a soothing and simple sound, one that is an almost shamefully effective bromide against all manner of doubt, and right now I am thinking that the devotée does not forget so exquisite a sound as his loved one's laughter, and that he can be forgiven should he commit the venial sin of forgetting some of the lesser delights, be they obscure beauty marks or the sounds of doors closing.

Such doubts about ownership eventually reduce themselves to the question of whether I belong here, for that is what ownership really is, the sense that you have of belonging to a place. By *belong* I mean belong as a pine does and as a palm does not. It is natural for the pine to grow here, unnatural for the palm; the one fits in the sense that it lives here unobtrusively and, relatively speaking, easily; the other would live here, if it could, flamboyantly. I will never fit as neatly into this acre as any of the trees I might pick out at random. Only when my flesh rots to feed the trees will I belong as completely as they do, and I can wait to achieve that kind of ultimate oneness with the earth. In the meantime, I aspire to live here as naturally and comfortably as men do anywhere on this earth, hoping, even though I belong to a species with one foot in and one foot out of the natural world, that in my presence here I can avoid the oppressive flamboyance of a palm, were one somehow to sustain life on these subarctic shores.

I liken myself to a small white pine we dug up to transplant near the camp kitchen the first year we were here. It is the only tree we have planted, the only tree that has ever received our special care. The rest live or die as they might, but this one we watered. There are still faint shovel tracks at its base, and the tree has a vague hothouse look to it, at least to my mind, perhaps only because I know its origin is on another shore. Nevertheless, it is a healthy, straight-stemmed tree with large bushy blooms of needles, and each year it looks more naturalized—more natural.

Both that tree and I are aliens, and we fasten ourselves to the land for much the same reason, because not to do so means death, literally for the tree, figuratively for me, because it is a form of slow spiritual atrophy to wander without ever belonging to a place. The roots that I send down are care, knowledge, and my presence here, whether for a week or, as now, for a summer, and my annual return sustains my care and expands my knowledge, which in turn feed the desire to return. I have discovered that just as my knowledge is never broader than when I am here, so is my care never greater than when the lock is off the door. Since ownership is a process and not merely a legal statement recorded in the proper place and manner, my claim to Nym, as anyone's would be, is like a squatter's, never more convincing than when I am here. Each year I willingly submit to living in the sphere of Nym's influence, just as the land exists (will, and thus submission, being irrelevant) under my influence, and the more I live here the better, the easier, the fit will be.

So, like the white pine, I fit—a little, and not as well as

most everything else here, and not as well as I will at the end of the summer or in five years or ten. But still, for now, a fit of sorts, and one that has improved in a matter of only weeks. Having wormed my way back by walking about reclaiming dimly remembered images, I belong here as much as I ever have—the lifting of my burdensome stiffness tells me that.

But the body may not be as intimately linked with the mind as I suppose, and it is possible that my stiffness was purely physical and that it simply exhausted itself as stiffness does and disappeared. Maybe I should look askance at the wonderful coincidence of finding a symbol, of all places, exactly where there ought to be one, and exactly where I looked. It could be that I have a hollow symbol on my hands and that I live under the delusion that I belong here. Except that last night after the last of the lingering twilight had disappeared, I followed the beam of my flashlight through the near blackness to the Toe where I went to check out the weather. I scanned all but the northernmost sky, which was hidden behind the trees, and after I had seen that all was clear, I stood for a few moments and gazed into the southern vault of the night sky. On the edge of vertigo from its clearly limitless depth, I turned toward the black curtain of trees, and as I walked into it I flipped on the switch to the light. The batteries were dead. Relying on memory and hunch to thread my way through the blackness, I found that I knew the narrow path as a man does the darkened rooms of his own house.

THE ORDER OF THINGS

Chapter Four

Earth, air, fire, water. Empedocles taught us 2,500 years ago that they are the stuff of the earth, the "roots of all." I believe him. In the Quetico it is easy to discount the chemist's periodic chart for its slavish literalness, and though Empedocles' cosmology is commonly thought to be outdated, I am partial to his schema because it is good poetry and transcends obfuscation. It is true that his world view wanders from the letter of things, but its simplicity mirrors the simplicity that undergirds this land, and his cosmology reflects the spirit of this country. Besides, a geography as lacking in dissemblance as this one deserves to be composed of four elements, not 105.

Because so little is hidden here, the Quetico is an excellent place to begin a study of geology. The most amateur of geologists can sleuth successfully here, since it takes neither the eye of a trained expert nor the imagination of a fevered poet to marry the explanations and descriptions in the guidebooks with the realities of the landscape. Basic knowledge is easily won, and the place makes sense because appearances do not deceive. A visitor here, wary of appearances, once looked down the steep scribbled shoreline and remarked offhandedly how Nym looks just like a hole filled with water. She was from southern Minnesota where sandy-shored lakes rest on the land like drops of water on a glass slide, and it took her a moment to realize how ridiculously right her passing comment had been. It is freakish to be granted such free access to reality, and she laughed at the absurd delight in having made such an obvious rediscovery.

It is the recent advance and retreat of a series of glaciers that have made the land as ingenuous as this. During the last geological epoch (the Pleistocene—2,500,000 to 10,000 years ago), Earth's climate cooled several degrees and snows in the region of what is now Hudson's Bay no longer melted. Piling up layer upon layer, the mass of snow became ice, and when it reached a thickness of 300 feet the body of snow and ice began to move. It had become a glacier. Spreading out like batter poured onto a griddle, it lumbered south over the Canadian Shield and into the Quetico at the rate of an inch to ten feet a day. By cementing uptorn rock debris into its snout and underbelly as it heaved down out of the North, the glacier quarried for itself cutting, scraping, gouging edges and planes that completely destroyed existing drainage patterns in its track, and the sheer weight of one of these icy leviathans, some of which grew to a thickness of two miles, flattened the crust of the earth. Nothing could stop the slow cataclysmic advance but a body of seawater or a rise in the mean temperature.

The fourth and last (but for the next) glacier met its end

due to a climatic change that occurred 15,000 years ago. The earth began to warm again and the glacier shriveling in the sun, began to retreat—or die—northward, losing its mass and leaving behind a barren profusion of scoured and tortured bedrock littered with gravel, rocks, and boulders, all awash in the melt-waters of rotting hulks of ice stranded like whales on a beach. The glaciers had stripped away intervening Earth history and left exposed a moonscape of Precambrian rock—rock of the same age as that buried at the bottom of the Grand Canyon.

Geologically speaking, the last advance of ice is today's front-page news. If, to add some meaning to the fantastic numbers involved, we telescope Earth's history into one year—now is the stroke of midnight on New Year's Eve—then the last glacier began its retreat less than fifteen minutes ago. Since this glacier made its exit only a quarter of an hour before our appearance, it is, of course, no surprise to find fresh tracks that are easy to read. The striated exposed rock surfaces were caused by the brush of rock against rock as the glacier moved south. The northeast-southwest grain of these elongated lakes, so obvious on a map of the Quetico, is the track left by the glacier as it furrowed its way across the land. The thin and ragged cover of soil is as telling as fresh paint that this is newly scoured land living out the first minutes of its latest incarnation. Even those strange spooky boulders at odd spots in the woods are attributable to the glaciers. Some of them are as big as three-story houses, and they wait almost expectantly, as if eons ago they were left behind for some obscure reason by traveling giants who will return for them in the next few days, hopefully not while you are around pondering one of them. The boulders are called erratics, lost out of the glacier as it made its melting retreat. This land is newly re-formed and undisguised, and if you cannot infer from its features that it was formed by a glacier, you need only read the word *glacier* or have it whispered in your ear, and the oddities and questions explain themselves.

If one chooses to trace local Earth history past the Pleistocene and back toward Earth's beginnings, there are, to be sure, obscurities enough to stump even the professional geologist. Yet he, just as much as the fair-weather geologist, is attracted to the Canadian Shield, and for much the same reason, though the professional studies beginnings here instead of endings. The Canadian Shield is unique among the great continental shields because of its vast expanses of exposed Precambrian rock, which by definition was formed after Earth cooled and before organic life had evolved to the point where it began leaving fossil traces. On the Shield geologists have access to Earth primeval, and they hope their study of these ancient rocks will fill in the missing chips in the mosaic of how Earth was formed. Yet, whatever the professional geologist eventually extracts from his study of the Shield, the events of the latest geological age are clear, and when we happen on simplicity it behooves us not to commit the unnatural act of burying it, and maybe ourselves, in a honeyhead of our own making. In the Quetico you can drop your defense against mere appearance. Each lake is the quintessential lake, like a Platonic form; whatever else a lake may be, whether it be spring-or rain-or snow-or stream-fed, it is at the least a hole filled with water.

The prevailing geologic mood is simplicity, and because we wish to fit here, we strive to maintain and emulate that simplicity. Clutter, either the appearance or the reality of it, is anathema here, and its nettlesome presence is to be watched for and swept away like a cobweb lest it mutate into chains. Therefore the cabin we would build had itself to be simple so that it would fit here. The obvious plan would have been to build a log cabin out of our own timber, but our land patent, which was only provisional until we had an enclosed structure, did not include the timber rights. But our lack of building experience would also have prevented us from building with logs. Having built nothing but the usual birdhouses and coffee tables in high school shop classes, we knew we were no more than wood butchers, and that it would be unwise to tempt providence by trying to build our cabin of anything but sized and finished lumber. But if not a log cabin, what?

If we were almost totally lacking experience in the building arts, then maybe it would make sense to clear our cabin site and then air-ferry in a factory-made metal trailer complete with carpeting and a brightly colored conical fireplace like the ones in the catalogues, or if not that, then to hire a carpenter who could help us with the design and who knew what he was about when it came to carpentry. No one even bothered, fortunately, to put forth the first suggestion, all of us agreeing without discussion that such gaucheness combines the drabness of a boxcar with the visual affront of an empty beer can as big as a boxcar. Aside from that, a man should be responsible for building his own house just as he is for washing his own body (and if idealism flags here, is there a chance for it anywhere?), a belief that also did away with the latter possibility.

We considered ordering from one of the lumber yards in Atikokan a prefabricated cabin, its pieces already cut out and numbered and ready to put together like a set of Tinkertoys or Lincoln-logs. There were objections to that, too. We wanted a cabin with our imprint on the design, and not that of some anonymous architect in Minneapolis or Miami who knew nothing of our wishes or needs; further, we wanted a cabin that was made to use and not only to sell. We would, we decided, design it ourselves and construct it ourselves, and if the product turned out to be more like a cartoon of a cabin, or if through inexpert workmanship or faulty design it collapsed the following winter, so be it.

How about an A-frame, then, one of our design and construction? someone asked. No. Its shape, though simple, is inefficient, and its simplicity is the kind that draws too much attention to itself. We were not here to out-Jones the Joneses by one-upping our neighbors the trees. A split-level, then, sided with plywood, something of modest design, but unique, tailormade for a special spot on the hill? Too ambitious, we knew, and we had come full circle, reminding ourselves again that we were anything but artisans.

During the months we spent considering various cabin plans through letters sent back and forth from Minnesota, Illinois, and Utah, Rick described for us a modernistic chalet he had seen once in the Swiss Alps. Three stories high and large enough to be a hotel, it was instead a private home. The chalet was rocked and timbered into the mountainside, and it clung there proudly—and, perhaps, precariously. Two sides of the living room fronted the valley, and massive, widely spaced beams were all that separated the main floor in the living room from the roof, which was three stories and thirty feet above. Windows on the valley sides of the chalet stretched the full height of the living room and offered an unobstructed and—need it be said?—sublime view of crag- and ice-encrusted Alps. Clearly the stuff of which picture postcards are made, I thought as I read, but what did this have to do with Northwoods cabins?

Rick suggested the outlandish, that this chalet, this modern-day castle, had just the sort of floorplan we wanted. Once it was stripped of its rich furnishings, its adornments, repetitions, and excesses, there was the basis of a building plan here that was simple and serviceable, and one that three apprentices could construct without benefit of a foreman. Rick roughed out the basic floorplan, and as we happily discovered in the next exchange of letters, we were all excited by the simplicity and efficiency the plan promised. In later correspondence and meetings we traded suggestions for changes and refinements, and after our consultations with those who had more experience than we, the sketches graduated to drawings and then to blueprints, which were neither blue nor orthodox but, for all that, still exact and readable by anyone. The final step in the preliminaries was to construct a balsa-wood scale model that included every detail except for the furnishings.

But we did not build the cabin first. We began with our outhouse, a two-holer (to spread the pile), which we built a couple of feet longer than necessary so that we could use part of it as a tool shed. We began with the outhouse first, not because we especially crave the creature comforts, but so that we might acquire experience where mistakes would not count so much. Our only error, committed late one afternoon while we were hurrying to finish measuring, cutting, and nailing on the siding, was to saw in two a section of the siding we had been saving for the express purpose of serving as our door. Sheepishly, we acknowledged what everyone is already supposed to know, that haste makes waste. In spite of our error, which turned out not to be so wasteful after all, since we were able to salvage the pieces for our door, when we finished we had an outhouse that was plumb and square, and what is more, the confidence that the following summer we could carpenter a cabin equally well built.

As planned, we returned the following summer and in two weeks of long days built the cabin. The scale model, which is just a toy now sitting on top of the bookshelf, assisted us in seeing how the parts were related to the whole, and we consulted it whenever our minds balked at thinking in three dimensions. Each night when darkness, or Suzanne's and Janet's call for dinner, forced us to take off our carpenter's aprons and stow our tools under the foundation, we would walk halfway down the path toward the kitchen and then turn to survey what we had built that day, and each time we were not a little surprised that we were the carpenters—yes, carpenters!—on that cabin which was so quickly going up. Again we discovered that patience, thoughtfulness, and planning can serve as effective substitutes for experience. A few stupidities committed in the act of construction resulted in some minor though negligible errors, and they were either removed or else expertly hidden. The only structural flaw that I have been able to detect—and that with the help of a plumb bob dangled from the roof peak—is that the roof leans a little to the northwest, but the list is so small that it is doubtful the laws of construction will exact any retribution for a good long while. Though there are some minor mistakes, the cabin is as simple and sturdy as we wished it would be, and we admit to being a little proud of our humble cabin.

The owner of the Swiss chalet, and probably his architect along with him, might regard their progeny as little more than a bastard child, and when we want to put on some false airs for the fun of it, we remind each other of the monied, high-toned lineage into which we arranged for our cabin to be born. The chalet reaches toward grandeur; our cabin would never be accused of that ambition, though perhaps of others. But, bastard or not, the cabin presents a face that more than her builders can love. It is well and lovingly made of high-quality, kiln-dried Canadian lumber. It is stout and steep-roofed and as strong as a seaman's chest. A perfect square twenty feet on a side, its cornerstone an outcropping of the Shield itself, the cabin rests on a foundation of eight additional cement pads topped with anywhere from one to four cinderblocks, according to what the terrain demands. The cabin is framed with pine and sheathed with aspenite, which is a particle-board pressed from aspen chips that is much used for building in this country, and it is capped with a traditional gable roof. Despite its plain, square, somewhat stubby look, we felt no need to jive it up by painting the exterior fire-engine red or banana yellow. We are partial to the color scheme that was in evidence when we arrived, and so we stained the cabin with a wood preservative that matches the rich, dark brown of wet jackpine bark, and we shingled the roof in forest green, except for a few strips at the peak where we ran out of forest green and had to finish with a lighter, dusty-green shingle.

The superstructure of the cabin is as ingenuous as the rock on which it rests. The skeleton is freely visible, and nothing is obscured or hidden by trim or finishing work. You can see how the frame of the cabin *works* to adjust and balance force and weight. Spacers have taken out the natural bows and small warps in the wall studs, thus perfecting their vertical rise and improving their parallel run, which in turn squares and strengthens the frame. Sheets of aspenite that cover the frame freeze its square lines into place. Horizontal ceiling joists, which span the cabin and are spiked into the rafters near the eaves, balance the outward thrust of the rafters, which at the roof peak lean into the ridgeplate. Vertical kingposts, which stretch from joist to rafter and form part of the roof trusses, relieve the rafters of some of the roof weight by distributing it onto the joists.

On the floorplan, identical sleeping alcoves—it would be pretentious to call them bedrooms—large enough for only a double bed and a small dresser sit at diagonal corners. At the other diagonal—but words are obscuring the lines:

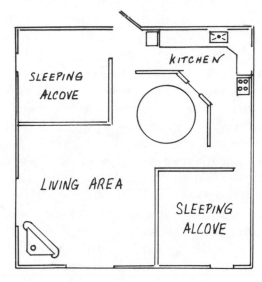

MAIN FLOORPLAN

Like the living room in the chalet, our living area is open to the roof, except for 2 six-by ten-inch beams that traverse it, and if our ceiling were not writ so small, we too would have what the developers call, whether it is writ small or not, a cathedral ceiling.

A ladder, which pulls out from storage against the north-east alcove wall, leads through a trapdoor above the dining area to the loft:

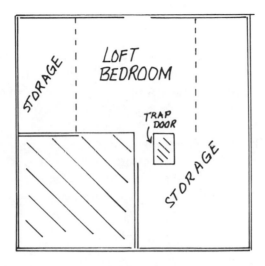

LOFT FLOORPLAN

A waist-high railing borders the loft overlooking the living area, and because the loft is not walled in at the kingposts, there is a pronounced spaciousness to it despite its modest dimensions. Bordering the loft behind the kingposts is ample storage—much more, in fact, than we are using.

There is an aesthetic to the design of this cabin, and the aesthetic is based partly on symmetry. It is a shining mystery why one's sense of the beautiful should resonate to the spatial rhythm that is called symmetry. We usually hold dear the rare rather than the commonplace, and spatial and aural rhythms are commonplace. Life begins when sperm and egg fuse after the rhythm of procreation; it ends when the rhythms of life-breath and heart-beat are broken; the interim is spent in a body outwardly symmetrical. Our lives are bound into rhythms as if they were the covers of a book and we were the pages, and it is a felicitous state of affairs, to say the least, that we harken to what there is so much of and that we seek even to create our own play of rhythms.

Rhythm is commonplace but seldom common, and thus it is that I am satisfied with—and by—the simple repetitions of the cabin: the two sleeping alcoves, identical in size and mirror images of each other down to their dropleaf windows; the two bay windows, each centered in a living room wall and equidistant from the focal point of the room, which is the Franklin stove sitting in the corner; the two kitchen windows, one an echo of the other, equidistant from the corner; the loft bedroom centered in the cabin between the two rows of six kingposts; and the loft window centered beneath the apex of the roof. Yet the symmetry of the cabin is not complete. There are grace-lines that save the cabin from a honeycomb tropism: the division of the cabin into fourths that are only approximate; the unbroken line of sight on only the one diagonal—from the kitchen, through the serving window in the dining area partition, to the living area; the open-ceilinged living room; the total dissimilarity between the loft and the main floor. Such contrapuntal lines as these rescue the design from the cold tedium of the hive.

We chose the design not only because it was simple, but because we saw in it the promise of function. The American sculptor and aesthetician Horatio Greenough equated the promise of function with beauty, and we tacitly accepted that part of Greenough's theory which states that an object is beautiful in proportion to how well it works. The form had to be adapted to the function, and each of our rooms is planned around its use. The sleeping alcoves might be considered tiny, even cramped, but they are expansive enough for two people to close their eyes and spend eight oblivious and restful hours. The small dropleaf windows, about the size of a common basement window, provide each alcove with good ventilation and light.

The kitchen is likewise designed around its use. It is not inefficiently strung out along one wall but is L-shaped, so that it wraps around the cook to cut inefficient and unnecessary movement (Frederick Taylor would commend us). The windows are near the most often used work areas, the stove and sink, and there is plenty of counterspace—more, in fact, than I have seen in many apartments. Underneath the counter are rough shelves where we keep our dishes in full view and within easy reach, and below them are our staples, all clearly marked in coffee cans or canisters. The kitchen side of the dining-area partition is shelved with scraps of wood, which provides us with additional storage.

Since the living area is where we spend most of our time, it is the largest room, of course, and the one where we most wanted to make efficient use of our limited space. Its open ceiling and the open line of sight into the kitchen combine to expand the room psychologically. The two large windows, which are screened at the bottom, provide sufficient ventilation and excellent light, even on cloudy days, and through each of them we have a fine view of the lake.

Except in the kitchen, the furnishings are as spare as the plan is uncomplicated. Strangely, we have three or four incomplete sets of dishes, sauce pans and stew pots and frying pans of every size, coffee pots for two and for twenty and for every size group in between. We could not serve an army—but probably a small church supper (and I suspect that many of these vessels have). But, aside from the surprising variety and number of dishes, we have: a bed and dresser, a mattress in the loft, a chair and couch, a treadle sewing machine housed in a wood cabinet, a small chair-side table, a kitchen table and chairs, and in the kitchen an icebox—the kind you put ice in—and a propane stove. And not much else.

It is because of a cloudburst yesterday afternoon that I have been thinking of the grooved lakes and the ragged carpet of fauna that has recently been rolled down here and the conscious simplicity we have tried not to lay on but to build into Nym. All day there was that nervous stillness that presages a storm, and an almost palpable mass of stagnant air lay over the land. Then in midafternoon there was the coming of the winds and after that the deluge itself, the sodden clouds splitting and spilling their torrent of water on the earth. From the window I watched, trying to part the curtain of water that hung from the eaves, and through it I caught glimpses of something I had never seen here before, and I was as startled as if I had seen a man suddenly appear from nowhere at the window. There was a stream of water running in my midst! The path to the Toe had become a rivulet of muddy water with a feisty current, and I traced its course down the hill and out of sight. Along its edges the wash of water had in a matter of only fifteen minutes formed alluvial fans and hillocks of pine needles, mud, and wood chips. "Je-sus," I swore under my breath, not because I had thought the country erosion-free, but because thoughtfulness and good intentions were not enough. While I stood there washed in the afterwaves of my own astonishment, I flashed into futures for Nym that were all full of the wrong possibilities and all of them my own doing—neon and concrete and steel and plastic and all things synthetic, dustbowls and amusement parks and ore trucks corkscrewing their way up out of a drained Nym Lake just as they are doing now out of Sleep Rock Lake not twenty miles away. The running sore out the window was at once an insult and an embarrassment and I was both resentful of and apologetic for it.

Can't I even walk on the land without gutting it? Maybe not: Acts have their consequences. If it does happen that without being aware of it in time, we immutably change or destroy what we have sought and found, we will, of course, not be unique. On the contrary. In Western culture that tradition dates back to Adam and Eve, who can be thought of as the patron saints of the destructive arts. Even in the Quetico we would not be unique, the fur traders and lumbermen having antedated us by a good many years. North Americans have demonstrated a miserably small capacity to husband their Eden. In fact, we have even had an ill time of it nurturing what we ourselves have built.

Rick, Bob, and I have some knowledge of the quiet paths that such destruction can take. That we built Nym is due largely to the fact that while we were in high school the three of us, along with nine others, built what in that Minnesota locale was called a hunting shack, which meant a sparsely furnished cabin not far different in conception from what I am living in now. Having decided that life was more worth living if you had a shack where you could hunt and try out your incipient adulthood with the guiding hand of parents and society resting a little more lightly than usual, we convinced one of our fathers to give us two rundown quonset huts that had at one time housed turkeys, and we transported them one at a time on a flat-bed trailer to a patch of soilbank that bordered a tree-lined pothole about ten miles from town. We had acquired squatters' rights there by politely asking the owner for them.

We tore out two ends and butted the quonsets together on a foundation of railroad ties, shoveled out the turkey droppings and disinfected the building with the strongest chemicals we could find, tar-papered the roof, replaced a few window panes and rotting boards, painted the inside and furnished it with a barrel stove and a table and some chairs. In a month we had our shack, and it was a simple, spare, and exciting place.

But we couldn't sit still. Pascal claimed that all man's troubles stem from his inability to sit still. That may not be an oversimplification. In our case, at least, he was right, literally right. With access to twelve basements and attics, we grew restless—we had discovered what a cornucopia of necessities each of them was, and we began to pick them over in search of items that would add further improvements to the shack. Various tools and cans of paint began to appear, and soon we had to partition off a tool room at one end of the shack in order to neatly house our excesses. It was discovered that we had enough baby-blue paint to cover the whole interior, so, of course, we were obligated to repaint. When we were done, everyone agreed that the new color was vastly superior to the old green, which was a vile shade that had looked old even when it was still wet—we had come by the green through chance, having had to mix all our paints together to get enough of the same color for one complete coat. Piece by piece additional furnishings began to appear, a medicine chest, a kitchen sink, a rollaway, some easy chairs, a double bed, an end table or two, even a battery-powered radio. Someone scrounged some carpeting, and what of the new flooring we couldn't use we stored under the shack, along with the overflow from the tool room. And so it went.

The winter of our freshman year in college we burned it to the ground. Our public reason for the burning was that, the group having split up and left home, the shack was ripe for usurpation by another set of squatters, underclassmen, whom we regarded as unworthy barbarians because they had not toiled as we had. The private and unspoken reason was that the burning signified our acceptance of the end of something, and what we burned on that bitterly cold Sunday afternoon was what many of us, I think, had ceased to want, and certainly what none of us had planned or foreseen three years before. The dirt and clutter had gotten the best of us, gotten away from us, and we had grown claustrophobic from all the clutter, which by imperceptible turns had grown more and more shabby and which in the end was only posing as comfort. In the alternating humidity and dust of the midwestern summer, the overstuffed furniture in the overstuffed shack had gone ratty with mildew. The rug zealously collected dust as if it had been laid for that very purpose, and the threadbare chair- and mattress-coverings clung to the skin like the sticky hot and vaguely verminous sheets off a sickbed. So it was with a measure of relief that we burned it, and afterward I regretted that one of the most noxious comforts could not disintegrate with the rest of them in that explosion of fire. Through the smoke near the charred railroad ties, I could still see a raw mound of dirt, the effluent from a landscaped patio that someone had begun to gouge from the hillside.

We met defeat once at the hands of restlessness, but now we have some idea of the nature of that sly continuum of acts that like a stagnant river appears innocent of movement, but that in time reaches the sea just the same. To single out this or that change as the most decisive or most important— acquiring our third hammer, for example, or laying the carpet—is as fruitless as trying to separate out the most important ten gallons of water in the river. Even assuming there is a decisive act, it is probable that our dull minds would miss it. It is like watching the hour hand on a wristwatch; we miss the movement because it is too fine and we see only the results. When you have come so far from the idea of a shack that you are considering wall-to-wall carpeting, the general course is clear even if its particulars are not, and the truly decisive moment—or, more likely, moments— is in that hazy, imprecisely plotted time when carpeting became a live possibility. Decisions are not made in a vacuum: They are made in the ambience created by the accumulation of past decisions. It pays to think of each act in the continuum as a vector that by definition has both direction and, what is most important—but only because we forget this so easily—momentum. Enough acts committed in the direction of complexity, and you are not only pointed in the wrong direction, you also have less chance, because of the combined momentum of events, of redirecting yourself.

It is hard to say at what point you ought to make your stand against the onslaught of clutter and complexity, but before your direction and momentum are glaringly obvious, and certainly before the innocent-minded willingly aid in the defense. If I am right, you must make an arbitrary and capricious judgment like the one I wish in retrospect I had made: No, it is absolutely crucial that we have only two hammers, not three. Such a pronouncement would have inspired all sorts of verbal abuse, and I would have been damned as ornery, arbitrary, a nitpicker, and—no doubt—a fool.

And my friends would have been right—it would have been a preposterous demand, and I would not argue that acquiring that third hammer was a watershed event. What I would argue, however, is that we could have suffered healthily under this delusion could we have been somehow convinced into believing it. Clutter grows like fire and it should be fought like fire. The practiced firefighter plows his firebreak at a safe, "arbitrary" point downwind of the fire to ensure that it will be contained. It is quibbling to argue that the firebreak be plowed exactly in the spot it is; it is not quibbling—in fact, it is crucial—to argue that a firebreak be cleared somewhere in that vicinity. The hammer is in the right vicinity, and so it is that I make a symbol of it and suppose that it had in it all the evils that were in reality spread through the continuum.

We now guard against the recurrence of the past and are more careful than we otherwise might be to sit still, and we have a certain trust and confidence in ourselves. We want, we say, to keep Nym simple. But I find myself wondering how far our trust in ourselves should reasonably extend. I see signs that we have begun to stir from our restfulness. I have said that the cabin is a wooden tent and that its lines are free, but that is not quite true, at least not any longer, not since we insulated and then, to cover the dirty-pink insulation, paneled the walls with a type of particle board often used for sub-flooring. We decided to winterize the cabin for the obvious reason that to do so would greatly extend its usefulness in this subarctic climate. Without insulation the Franklin stove did keep the cabin at a temperature hovering somewhere between the bearable and comfortable marks, but the certitude of comfort that insulation provides will encourage us to use Nym more in the winter. It is also true that in deciding to insulate we had our collective eye turned toward the future—that part of it just beyond what is called the foreseeable future—when each of us hopes to realize the wish to winter here. If we grant ourselves the wish, a winterized cabin would be, if not a necessity, indistinguishable from it.

We have increased the utility of Nym by improving it, and to my surprise the addition of insulation and paneling has not diminished the uncommonly large psychological space that we have managed to fit into these modest dimensions. My surprise is welcome, but at the same time it gives me pause to question how accurately we can predict the effects of future improvements. In this democratically run cabin, the decision to insulate was unanimous—enthusiastically so, in fact—but I wonder how controlled the step really was. The framing is now hidden by the paneling, and I miss—more than I thought I would—the strict geometrics of the wall studs bisected by the spacers, and I miss the feeling of being not much inside—or inside by only a three-eighths-inch thickness of aspenite. Because of a shortage of insulation we have not yet insulated the roof, so its lines are still free, but I wonder whether when the rafters are closed off, our improvement will not muddy to oblivion the music of rain beating on the roof. But if it does, maybe I won't miss the music.

There are other signs of our refusal, or maybe our inability, to sit still for very long. Gone are the days when against my will I tried to decipher the cranky metaphysics of a succession of fitful and failing outboards. A couple years ago we invested in a fine, new ten-horse outboard, which thus far has been exactly what we wanted it to be, the *ne plus ultra* of dependability. There is now talk of replacing our battered boat with a new and deeper one, the argument being that our present one is not so much old as dangerously shallow for a lake the size of Nym. To have to rely on this boat for transportation, especially in autumn winds so stiff and steady they seem machine-made, is to be imbued with the forcefulness and essential rightness of that argument. But if we purchase a boat, we also ought to replace the primitive boat slip at the Toe with a more permanent dock. I have noticed that on some days the boat edges toward the Toe and ever so lightly brushes against it, and some of the rivets near the transom are being ground away. We would certainly not want to subject a new boat to similar treatment, and the construction of a dock, properly lined with old car tires, would not be a luxury so much as a simple act of preventative maintenance. The dock, however, would advertize our presence here, which would defeat our having set the cabin back in the woods as insurance against being rifled by latter-day Vandals, who pillage even around here these days. At one time we considered adding a porch, but we discovered that the cabin is sufficiently cross-ventilated. Having given up on the porch, we now think of building a sauna, which would, admittedly, be a summer luxury—but it would also be a winter necessity. I have even picked out a tentative site bordering the clearing behind the Toe, and I know just how the runway of two-by-ten-inch planks will extend from the sauna door to the Toe and the restorative icy waters beyond. Thinking about it, I can almost feel the assaulting waves of dry heat from the water-spattered red-hot rocks and that delicious plunge into the water that purges body and mind of sundry discomforts. It will be hard, I know, to get along without that sauna.

As it will be hard to get along without the boat and the dock and the succession of other necessities that, apparently, will from time to time come looking for us to present their wares for our consideration. Such improvements are like people, individually agreeable, but who in the aggregate sometimes turn uncontrollable. Though many of these necessities will prove quite attractive, it remains to be seen whether we will succumb to their individual blandishments. But even now—fortunately now—it is a tiresome thought to consider the stewardship involved in keeping track of and maintaining an increase in wealth and complexity. We do not want to be stewards of a concoction of clutter, and improvements, if they are not improvements enough, will point us in a direction and spawn a momentum we never intended. So we are wary, but in a healthy and not a pathological way, of our direction and speed, and we choose to go, if at all, slowly.

It may be, of course, that we have no ultimately efficacious control over the character which this cabin assumes. Civilizations arc said by some to have a life span in the same way that a sexually reproducing plant or animal does. Death is a built-in fact of life, and it may be the same with our cabin. I look up at the roof and it suggests just that. It is steep-pitched so that its lines will relieve it of the weight of winter snow and so that we could include a loft. But there is another reason for that steep pitch. If we ever need extra storage or sleeping space, we can, with a minimum of trouble, simply raise the roof and add a dormer. When I consider this last option that we have reserved for ourselves, I wonder if we haven't designed into the cabin the obsolescence of its simplicity. It is as if we have subconsciously anticipated the certain appearance of clutter, which is the prodigal that without fail returns and for which we have prepared a place, not because we love it, but because we recognize it as family.

Maybe it is illusion that our experience with the shack will ever be of any real benefit. But until convinced otherwise, I have to believe that experience is worth more than to forestall the inevitable. Yet, even though I cast my lot with experience, I would not want to rely on it exclusively to save us from our own tinkering. Fortunately, there is help proffered from other quarters.

Sloth, traditionally considered one of the seven deadly sins, may not prove so deadly here. In fact, she may be our guardian angel. At least she is working for me now. There are a number of small improvements that I have scheduled for myself this summer, and one of them is to hook up a trap and drainage line to the kitchen sink so that we will be spared the inconvenience of having to dump a potful of slops after doing the dishes. Even though it has been four years since Rick and I dug the outhouse hole, I have had enough of digging for a while yet, and the task of hooking up the line and burying it remains undone. I just haven't gotten around to it. And I don't really expect that I will unless boredom or a new wave of Puritan guilt gets the best of me some afternoon.

I have my reasons. Sinks are generally thought to be unworkable—worthless—unless they are fitted out with a drainpipe, but because of our hurry to use the sink once it was permanently installed in the kitchen counter, we temporarily placed under it one of those huge pots that had once served in a church kitchen, and we were quickly disabused of the error that a sink requires a drainage line to be useful. Our sink is a marvel of simplicity. When I pull the plug the water swirls down into the pot, and then I carry it outdoors and dump it in a natural depression about fifty feet from the cabin. There is no pipe to drain or to take in each fall and put out each spring; there is no pipe to clog and no plunger or plumber's snake necessary to unclog it. The drainless sink is error-free and bother-free, and I for one am willing to carry out the slops to maintain the best of all possible worlds, which in this case is the convenience of a large and permanent sink combined with the positive luxury of knowing that the sink will never be the source of any irritation whatever. A sink with a drainage line is not only not a necessity; it is a bogus convenience I can do handsomely without.

But having said that, I myself am not entirely convinced by this justification for laziness. That is, I believe the argument, but only a little—probably because it is a bit shrill and tries too hard. But if I were persuaded by my own argument any more than I am, my laziness would lose its purity, and, in any event, I know that procrastination and my disinclination to putter, and not this rationalization for my nonaction, are carrying the day and keeping me from adding one more worthless convenience.

My tongue is in my cheek? Maybe a little, but only insofar

71

as I am contrary enough to enjoy being saved by a deadly sin like sloth. That personal quirk, however, should not obscure the fact that a little more mindless laziness mixed with all that mindless activity in our high school days would have at least checked the clutter which eventually encrusted the place, and sloth can do the same for us here.

Supposing that every other defense fails to save us from ourselves, there is one last defense, and that is Nym's isolation. It may be the best defense of all. Having been required to build a cabin here to obtain our land patent, we are homesteaders of a sort, and we like to think of ourselves as such, but it would be foolish to try, as those in whose tradition we follow, to wring a living from this mean land. Though it is not strictly accurate to say that the land is trapped out and logged out, practically speaking it is true when you own a mere acre of it and when the government has finally begun to husband what it had before only administered. As for gardening or farming, the land was gutted long ago by the glaciers and is now a wasteland, agriculturally speaking, though a starkly beautiful one. Thus we are not tempted to live here permanently, reality having effectively quashed that dream even before it had a chance to be dreamed. As long as we are transients, as long as we have great distances to travel to reach Nym, and as long as we have only a limited time to tinker, Nym may be safe in—and from—our hands. For now, we can still say of Nym that it is composed of earth, air, fire, and water.

HOUSEWIFERY

Chapter Five

Pascal is reputed to have said that little things console us because little things afflict us. He might have said—and I would be more sure of this—that little things satisfy us because they afflict us. Today, for instance, it is housewifery that satisfies me. Midmorning now: Out front, sheets drying on the clothesline slap in the wind that is driving in off the lake; in the oven, white beans that soaked the night now bubble in a sauce of molasses and salt pork, perfuming the air with a meaty sweetness; on the chopping block in the lee of the cabin, two loaf pans of bread dough sit in the sun for their last rising. I hang the dishcloth on its nail and pour a cup of coffee from the thermos, then sit at the table to roll a cigarette. Things are complete, or they soon will be once the loaves are cooling on the counter, and I am satisfied.

I am satisfied because once again I have done away for the time being with those small afflictions, the cooking and cleaning, that accompany all but the most brutish existence. I can squeeze some small pleasure out of the sight of a floor freshly swept or a rack of dishes dripping dry, the steam still rising off the topmost pans, and I count myself fortunate in knowing the reward in the fact of a task completed.

There are quite a number of those tasks to complete, and my chores take me longer to complete, comparatively speaking, than they do today's average householder. There is water to be hauled up the hill from the lake; the wash to be scrubbed on the washboard, then rinsed two, three, even four times and wrung by hand, then hung to dry; wood to be sawn, split, and stacked; the fireplace to be cleaned of its accumulated ash and blacked against rust—and so the list goes. I am not very well applianced to carry out my chores, my only conveniences being a gas range converted to propane and a can opener of the antique hand-crank variety. The icebox I had to give up, at least as an icebox, because of the difficulty in keeping it stocked with ice, and now I use it as a linen chest. To replace the icebox I built an evaporation cooler which hangs suspended from a birch sapling I lashed between two pines that stand in front of the north kitchen window. The cooler is nothing but a screened box with a pan of water on top. Towels, which are supposed to act like giant wicks, hang down out of the pan of water over the screening, and the theory is that a breeze will blow through the wet toweling and cool the contents of the box. Sometimes, though, I wonder if the cooler would work at all without my faith in the principle of evaporation as I have applied it. There is no icebox or washing machine, no electricity or plumbing, and not even a hand pump or a drain in the sink, but of course we have no one to blame but ourselves for this sad state of affairs since we intentionally designed and built our house to be substandard.

Since I spend as much time at it as I do, it seems only prudent to get the most out of housewifery that I can. Yet, having so frequently gleaned the rewards of a task completed, I am pleasantly surprised that I have not grown weary of the compensations of domestic life. One reason I can still enjoy the chores is that I am careful about how I spend my labor. In a word, I am no spendthrift. Fortunately I was not trained from childhood to search out dirt like a police dog sniffing for explosives, and my lack of training has been advantageous since some things, at least, should be taken for granted, and a certain amount of dirt at the edges of one's life is one of them. Too much zeal has been misdirected toward dirt, and I am determined not to waste whatever zeal is in me on so inconsequential a problem. So I did not bother this morning to boil my sheets or even to heat the water or to put bleach in it. As a result, the sheets hanging on the line now are not whiter-than-white, but as I have said, I am no zealot and do not expect miracles from a wash tub. The sun is all the bleach I need, its price is never inflated, and though my sheets are merely a bright and solid white and thus not fit for angels, I would not be embarrassed to let any mortal sleep in them.

It is not my calling to root out dirt from my life, so instead of going in search of dirt, I let it find me out, and when it does I then decide whether the effort to rid myself of it will be reasonable. Sometimes, as with the braided rug that used to cover the living room floor, the effort is unreasonable and I do away with the cause altogether. The rug collected pine needles and wood chips like a magnet drawing iron filings, and the rug is too unwieldy for one man to easily haul outside and hoist onto the clothesline for a good beating with a broom. The only way I knew to clean it was to go down on my hands and knees and give it a kind of dry scrubbing with a stiff whisk broom. But such labor is extremely tedious and out of all proportion to the luxury, if that is what it was, of having a rug beneath my feet, so I rolled up the rug and stowed it behind the couch.

Rather than forgoing one small enjoyment, I discover that

in giving up the rug I have really traded one benefit for another—and one that this time is free. A rug ravels the edge of every sound—how much I did not know until I rolled up the rug—and now I can listen to the clean, taut sounds that fill my rugless rooms. The emptiness augments mere noise to the higher value of individualized sounds, like the tinkling of a spoon as it strikes the side of an empty bowl, almost a chime, or the snare-drum brush of Zip's nails clipping quickly across the wood whenever I give a low whistle for her. Such sounds I had never properly heard before, and I delight in them, much more so than I ever did in the rug.

Neither is it worth my while to wash the windows. They are clean enough. Since Nym is far from any of civilization's great smog centers, we have none of that yellow scum in the air that smears itself like wax onto the windows. Here there is only a little airborne dust and some cobwebs, and if you give it a chance the wind will sweep them away in good time. Besides, there are things to see in the webby windows.

Outside in the upper corner of the window that fronts the sink, there is an orb-weaver spider who keeps well hidden, coming out of her corner only for repair work when the wind damages her web. The first time I saw the web I was doing dishes, and I put down a soapy plate so that I could search out the best of those secret lights by which to trace the delicate symmetry of her web. As I was marveling at its radiating lines, a horsefly buzzed into this beautiful silken trap and was caught, and I watched the spider hobble out of her corner toward the scream of her prey. With silk from her spinnerets she bound the wings that fanned furiously only inches from my eyes. The wings shackled and at last mute, the spider mounted the fly and stung him with her venom, then retreated to her corner to wait. Within the minute she again came out along the same silken strand and humped her body over his, nuzzling the fly as she did so, as if she had reconsidered and would caress her captive out of his stupor. I moved even closer to see what she was doing, and as I watched, my nose almost pressed to the glass, her sides pumped and she slowly, and with much love, sucked him dry. Sated and her body fat with the life-juice of the fly, she then wove her way back to her dark corner—and I stood aghast at this small murder that had been so enlarged by my closeness to it. If this was Mother Nature, I thought as I watched the spider settle into what looked like slumber, she was more than red in tooth and claw, she was a bitch, and I wanted to destroy the web and disown my matronage.

Or at least that was how I first viewed the scene framed in the kitchen window. My horror did not last for long and now I am no longer repulsed, partly, I suppose, because I have gotten used to both the idea and the presence of the spider. It happens that she has picked a particularly fine spot to spin her web; this morning, for instance, I counted three papery carcasses, all huge horseflies, hanging in the net as it pulsed in the eddy of the wind. The spider was sleeping, or perhaps hibernating, in her corner as usual. But I have not simply grown jaded through repetition of what I once saw as a bestial—but above all—strange act. Something happened that forced an enlargement of my views.

One warm afternoon a few days after I had witnessed my first fly being eaten, I was bent over the porch step, paint brush in hand, restaining the worn boards. I was doing my best to hurry because the horseflies were tormenting me in that devilish way they reserve for specimens of humanity. Knowing somehow within their genes the sites on my back that were out of range of my hand, they were indulging themselves in an orgy of biting and chewing, and as I worked the bites became—as they always do—meaner and more personal. Quickly bitten into vengeful frustration, and my anger inflamed all the more by the very smallness of my foe, I demanded vengeance. I retrieved a club-sized length of one-by-four from underneath the cabin and I began to stalk the flies. When one would land near the corner of the cabin, I would slam the board at the fly, feeling a rush of venomous delight whenever I succeeded in splattering innards on the cabin wall, and the deaths, punctuated and thus made more significant by the mad bangs of wood on wood, did in some measure appease my anger.

After seven or eight kills my bloodlust finally fell below the boiling point—and I looked up to see in her corner the spider, with whom I now realized I had allied myself. The spider and I were not so different after all. Or perhaps we were—my death-dealing was quicker but marred by passion—and my squeamishness over how she takes her meals was nothing but ignorance, even arrogance, a form of provincialism that is ultimately at odds with my stated desire to live here modestly. Suddenly grown sheepish at the sight of my own carcasses festooned from the walls, I saw that the spider is no crone, no bitch—if we are to pass out such judgments, I fit those terms much more nicely. Her acts are not murders: She only eats. Now when I watch the spider come out of her corner, I think of her—if it is a her—as about to sit down to a bowl of warm oatmeal, as I myself might do. With her airy web the spider has brought into bold relief what should always be self-evident but what is so thoughtlessly, even willfully disregarded: Excepting at the expense of my own existence, each form of life has the right, simply and necessarily by virtue of its existence, to go on being itself. The web stands as a discourse on this ideal of tolerance and benevolence, and the homily that I have extracted from out of the kitchen window is easily expanded past the smallness of spiders. So the windows are a bit dirty because I prefer to leave the spider to her life, and I have no

plans to wash them soon. Besides, who knows what other
sights wait in the windows?

I have my reasons for neglecting some of the usual chores
like window washing and rug cleaning, and though I carefully
husband my labor, I do not mean to suggest that it is never
willingly spent. It is true that as recently as two months ago
the rewards of the householder were still as well hidden from
me as they had been all my life. Having had more than
enough personal experience with housewifery to form a solid
opinion of it, I agreed with the prevailing wisdom that
whatever satisfactions there were in it had to be essentially
negative, of the sort I get, for instance, when I mislay my
ideal of tolerance and kill off three or four mosquitoes in one
swat because it is more efficient than simply shooing them
away. But I have changed my opinion on the matter of
domestic tasks, and I no longer view them as holding actions
that can only be stoically tolerated at best. Now I more than
tolerate the chores; I look forward to them, not only to their
accomplishment but to the doing itself. There is even
something aesthetic about the new whiteness of a scoured
sink or the squeak of flesh as my finger trips and skids its way
across the hot wet metal of a pan just rinsed.

Such a view is unpopular, I admit, or at least the expression of it is, and one individual was so outraged by it to
suggest, not really facetiously, that I ought to apologize for
such an atavistic opinion, or at the least not admit to holding
it. Today housewives are reminded by those who have
ascended to a higher consciousness that it is a small mind
indeed which finds satisfaction in the humble, endlessly
repetitive domestic tasks, and the vanguard counsels that
such rewards—if they exist at all—are not worth holding
onto. No one, of course, cares to have his intelligence

impugned, so where the chores are concerned, the fact accomplished cannot be "the sweetest dream that labor knows," as Robert Frost said of physical labor. For house-keepers, there can be no such sweet dreams.

If this be the case, one might suppose that I have let myself in for especially numbing drudgery, since Nym is set, domestically speaking, somewhere in the nineteenth century. Given Nym's backward setting, and given the oft-repeated warning about the occupational disease to which I am susceptible, I am of course on the lookout for signs of mental barrenness, which is the lot of the housewife just as black lung is of the coal miner. Even though self-diagnosis is medically suspect, I will venture to say that I have not become a drudge; in fact, Nym's century has led me out of drudgery instead of into it. I am practicing housewifery in a new time—or at least in a time new to me, which is the same thing—and I find that daily life here is a lesson in history. Until this summer I knew nothing of my great-grand-parents—not so much as their names—and little enough of even my grandparents, but now I know much about them. My knowledge is different from that of the genealogist who from the ledgers of church and state copies out the names and relations, the dates of births and deaths, marriages and christenings, comings and goings. My province is private history, the in-between times, and without that knowledge the genealogist's thin citation of public doings strikes me as only a cipher.

Hardly a day goes by that I do not recover some arcane item out of that store of common knowledge which is largely lost to the present generation. My grandfather, if he smoked, likely never knocked a live coal from his pipe down a dry outhouse hole, as I—who absent-mindedly mixed up my centuries and assumed porcelain-and-water plumbing—did one of those first days in June, wondering as I watched the bright jewel smolder in the gloom next to the timbers shoring the outhouse whether to run for a bucket of water. It is not easy to explain my violation of the commonest common sense of another time. Some things, such as the small range of possibilities given fire and wood, can accurately be guessed at, but constant vigilance is also required to ensure that disaster will be averted. I can say only that it is tedious and wearing to be always vigilant, and that my wits strayed for a moment. But now, having been apprised of how easily the bathroom can burn, I keep my wits about me as closely as I suppose Grandfather kept his.

I am learning the other once-public secrets of fire, and I have come by a new appreciation for the knowledge of past generations. As it happens, I am a direct benefactor of Benjamin Franklin's genius. A true cast-iron model of his stove warms and comforts me from its station in the corner between the wide windows. Until we bought our used Franklin, which we got at a bargain price without even having to bargain, I was somewhat puzzled that this stove was still being manufactured, unless to satisfy those people who buy them to accessorize, as I believe the word is, a den or living room done up in the Early American style. But having lived with the stove under all conditions, I know how perfectly reasonable it is to demand that this stove function as more than a mere conversation piece. I have discovered it to be a very functional and versatile stove. If, on a warm night, I want the comfort of a fire without the heat, I have only to leave the stove doors open. On colder nights when I want the cabin heated rather than my imagination fired, I can trans-form the stove into a furnace by stuffing it with wood—it seems to make little difference if some of it is green, damp, or rotting—close the doors, and then lock them before all the wood can fall out onto the stove fender. Lying in bed on cool nights with the stove stuffed full, I can hear air being sucked into the vents at the bottom of the doors, and the relative loudness of that bass hum tells me how hot and fast the furnace is burning and whether my alcove will soon be too hot for sleeping.

I have learned to contend with almost all the variables in heating the cabin, and now I can regulate the heat almost as evenly as if the stove were equipped with a thermostat. According to the wind conditions and the outside and inside temperatures, I know when to shut the doors and when to open them up, how far to stop down the damper and air vents, what kind of wood to use and how much, whether it should be squaw wood or logs, split or unsplit, pine or aspen. Some of what I know goes deeper than words, or at least deeper than my ability to describe it. What is it exactly that tells me the log you are sawing will be too long for the stove grate? Yet I would never shy away from making such a prediction, and what amazes me at least as much as it would you is that I will be right.

Not that I have exhausted what my grandfather probably knew about stoves. Having used it in all conditions, I know the great versatility that Franklin designed into his invention, but it is not quite a stove for all weathers—or perhaps the problem is that I am not a fireman for all weathers. On those still, fog-dark days when the air is so thick it seems you could wring the heaviness out of it, the stove does not draw as well as usual, and after I build a fire in it I usually have to wait a few teary-eyed minutes until the tongues of smoke, which on those days are as heavy as lava, at last begin to struggle skyward up the pipe instead of flowing out across the floor.

A couple weeks ago when Rick was here for a few days of rest from farming, we built a big fire in the stove and closed the doors to wait for the coals so we could smoke some fish, and as we talked I chanced to look at the stovepipe, which runs straight up from the stove through an asbestos-lined firestop-box set into the cabin roof. Our blast furnace in the corner seemed to be blowing harder than usual, and in the failing late afternoon light the pipe looked almost as if it were beginning to glow a dim red. Wondering whether our senses were deceiving us, we went outside to see whether anything was amiss up on the roof, and once out the door we could hear a strong hollow roar of wind in the direction of the chimney. As we rounded the corner of the cabin we looked up to see flames—flames!—shooting out from beneath the weather cap on our single stack.

Chimney fire! that's what this was!—without words we made the discovery simultaneously. While Rick pulled the ladder out from beneath the cabin, I raced back inside, almost tearing the screen door from its hinges, and shut down the air vents and damper on the stove, hoping that I could starve the fire that was apparently raging up the whole twenty feet of stovepipe and chimney. But, as often happens with theories, this one needed more ideal conditions than the moment provided to prove out. The stove was obviously not as airtight as I had thought, and the fire raged on, burning now as if the whole room had become a bellows blowing air into it. There was no question now that the pipe was red-hot.

Meanwhile, pine needles that had lodged next to the chimney on top of the firestop-box—I had always thought that was so picturesque—had burst into flames, and Rick was on the roof hollering to all the world for water. Carrying our bulky eight-gallon fire pump up the ladder was out of the question, as I quickly discovered—the pump had handles, or rather symbols of them, and they obviously had been designed by someone who had never considered the possibility that this pump might actually have to be used. Forced to give up on the pump, I next tried to fill a collapsible canvas bucket from the pump, but the bucket persisted in collapsing, even with water in it, so I was reduced to holding the bucket upright with one hand while I tried to cradle the pump under the other arm and pour water from the pump into the bucket. The miserable effectiveness of this method— but not my panic—can be easily imagined, and it took me weeks to get a full bucket of water.

By then the fire had spent itself. To feed our illusion that we had had something to do with putting it out, we threw a few perfunctory buckets of water onto the chimney and marveled at how it spat and steamed. Our firefighting—what of it there was—had actually been done in the construction of the cabin. We were fortunate to have built so well. The firestop-box and the steel stovepipe—we might have used tin pipe and a simple metal shield—had contained the heat, so at least one of our theories had held up to the test of the real world. We had only mopped up the fire, or to be more precise, swept up, since our only contribution at the time of the fire was Rick's sweeping the flaming needles from the roof with his boot. The rest was not much more than bluster.

Later, after Rick had left and I was alone again, I wondered what my grandfather might have done in our circumstances. The dull red pipe would probably have been enough sign that he was in immediate danger of being burned out, but I decided that it was unlikely that he had ever found himself in our circumstances. In his day people did not have to wait for a chimney fire of their own to be convinced that such a fire is a possibility, even a near certainty if you happen, as we do, to burn wood with a high pitch content. A few unfortunates or fools always provided everyone else with vicarious experience of chimney fires, and it was because of such socially useful people that chimney fires were part of the common knowledge and experience of past generations. From the example of others, my grandfather knew enough—I am assuming he was a sensible man—to give a look up the stovepipe every once in a while to see whether it needed to be swept of the creosote that builds up there eventually to turn the chimney into a gigantic and unpredictable blow torch. I, however, do not benefit from my grandfather's common sense, and though I had heard the term *chimney fire*—by which I mean only that I knew there was such a thing—the term lay buried in that heap of forgotten words, once heard of—as I had heard of trolls—but never met with vicariously or otherwise and hence forgotten because it was never really known in the first place. Without someone else to play the fool, it is likely that you will get to play the part yourself much of the time. But, even though experience is a frustratingly unsystematic teacher who is perfectly willing to let us act the fool, she is at the same time a highly effective teacher since her lessons are graphic, even personal—much more yours because her offering is shinier and more valuable than some worn piece of information bestowed upon you by a mere man—and therefore her lessons are not easily given up.

Now I, too, have acquired my grandfather's sense, and fire is no longer the potential enemy it was—or rather, I am a new respecter of that potential. In fact, I would say that my sense of its potential is even more solid than my grandfather's—that is the compensation for those who need to learn by experience—since mine is not based on anything as impersonal as hearsay or common sense. Having had a fire, I can acknowledge that fires are sometimes pleased to break out where it is inconvenient to fight them, and I can recognize the utility in being able to appear, if not in two places at once, then—more realistically—in first one place and then *immediately* in another. So, besides reminding myself that the stovepipe needs to be kept free of debris, I have made arrangements to move quickly and surely if—it is really safer to say *when*—there is a fire, and I keep a ladder leaning in readiness against the eaves so that I can carry it upright to wherever it is needed. I have also cured the canvas bucket by soaking it in the lake to restiffen it, and until we can buy a proper back pump with a hose and nozzle, I will at least know that the canvas bucket can stand alone when it must.

Once there were strict divisions of labor, and my grandmother had her own store of secret knowledge, much of which was denied my grandfather by reason—if it can be called that—of his maleness. There being no divisions of labor in this society, I am having out of necessity to learn my grandmother's secrets, yet it is also true that I am probably more eager to learn them than my grandfather might have been since society did not permit him my curiosity about the traditionally female tasks. Even though it is said that undivided labor is inefficient labor, I am glad enough to hoard all the labor for myself because, being curious about household matters, I am naturally interested in expanding my knowledge in whatever directions I can. Bit by bit I am relearning my grandmother's skills and recovering her lost knowledge. I have learned, for instance, that eggs will keep a week and more at room temperature if the shells are not cracked, that canned tomatoes, once opened, will spoil more quickly than a cut fresh tomato. I know that a green pepper will rot in three days at room temperature. I know, despite the directions given on the back of the can, the proper way to black a stove, and I can clean a lamp globe without simply rearranging the patterns of soot. Many such rudiments of my grandmother's life must have been done so often as to sink beneath her mind and into the bones themselves. Though this morning I had to run over somewhat methodically the list of possibilities of where I could leave the bread dough to rise, my grandmother would have known somewhere beneath knowledge that this morning the chopping block would be the best place. Living as she did without a hot-water tap, she would never have forgotten—it would be inaccurate, except in the loosest sense, to say that she would have *remembered*—to set the dishwater to heat on the stove before eating so that she would have hot water when the meal was over. But then I no longer forget that either, some of these things, as I say, being done so often as to acquire the force of instinct.

Living without the usual amenities has served to firm up my opinion of them, and I have come to consider myself something of an expert on them. After all, if you wanted to study the advantages of having hair, the best person to ask would not be a man with a full head of it, his experience being rather narrow. Often I have wondered whether electricity is really the necessity it is thought to be. One man's luxury, of course, can be another's necessity, and in the present generation there are probably those who would seriously question my evaluation of electricity—I am disregarding at the outset the disputatious who simply love a good argument. I am more certain, however, that my grandparents would agree with me that, in comparison to some of the other benefits of electricity, electric lighting is so negligible a benefit as to be downright paltry.

I get along nicely with a kerosene lamp. The general impression of kerosene lamps seems to be that when it comes to serious lighting, they are impossibly quaint, their only purpose in our day being to provide an old-timey atmosphere that will complement the major accessories like spinning wheels and Franklin stoves. I do most of my reading and mending next to the window in natural light, and I find that I can easily work into dusk without any artificial light at all. When I do light the lamp I am surprised at how easy it is to work by kerosene flame. There is no softer or more restful light, and what it lacks in quantity is easily made up for in quality. True, my kerosene lamp will not flood any of my rooms with light, except my sleeping alcove, but that is rarely necessary anyway, and when it is, I light the gas lamp, which hisses its harsh light into every corner. But I much prefer the kerosene flame for its softness and silence.

Of course there are some drawbacks to a kerosene lamp. It is something of a fire hazard, but, as with the chimney, acknowledging the hazard greatly lessens it. The lamp globes must be cleaned every three or four days, yet that is no longer a nuisance since I discovered that soot smudges can be easily removed simply by polishing the globe with a piece of newspaper. It is also true that I can no longer command the light to appear, as I was used to doing, by simply flicking a switch, but I am not so lazy that I will complain about the hardship of striking a match. If it were suddenly discovered that light bulbs were somehow doing irreversible and serious damage to the environment, I for one would not long mourn their banishment.

I do not mean to suggest, however, that the world was cursed when it went electric. If I were a mother doing the week's wash for her family, perhaps I would think of electricity, along with the washing machine that is powered by it, as gifts from the gods on the same par with fire. Doing my wash is as close as I have come to drudgery at Nym. On cool mornings after the wash is hung to dry, my hands have at times been numb enough, my back sore enough to suggest to me how grueling that chore might become had I more than myself to wash for. Before I should want my house heated or lit with electricity, before I should want an electric water heater or water pump—cold, hand-pumped water will do—I should want electricity to power a washing machine. I feel sure that my grandmother, at least, would agree with my order of priority. I am less sure about my grandfather. If I hear protestations from him, I attribute them to the fact that, unlike my grandmother, he probably had only an imperfect acquaintance with bar soap and the ribs of a washboard.

Housewifery

In recovering this knowledge I move back to the sources of things and I am able to correct certain small inaccuracies and distortions in my views of things. I would say, in fact, that I am being enlightened. When I was in high school someone told me that words and languages have histories. That possibility had never occurred to me before. By turns the idea was preposterous, strange, fitting, then entirely natural—everything else had a history: why not words, too? For some reason I was vaguely incensed that there was such vast ignorance about the histories of even common words, and I remember setting about rather haphazardly to expunge some of this ignorance, at least in myself, by looking up etymologies of the commonest words I could think of. In somewhat the same way as when I was in high school, I am again confronting a pool of ignorance within myself. Just as there are etymologies hidden in even common words, there are histories in the common items everywhere in my house, and I have been trying to puzzle some of them out. Pickles, for instance. I had never considered the possibility that pickles might have an etymology, but so they do. I had never given them more than a passing thought—that thought being that dill were good and sweet were not. Pickles were a condiment everyone could afford, a relish, a delicacy, and therefore hardly a food at all, like the lettuce underneath the fruit salad. If something so insignificant as a pickle could be said to have an actual purpose, I supposed that its function must be to titillate jaded palates.

That, at least, was what I thought in the days when I ate pickles only on Thanksgiving and Christmas, and—more importantly—in the days when I had a refrigerator. But there is more to pickles than was meeting my rather narrow modern eye. Now I eat three or four pickles a day, fat polski ogorkies, and if I had to classify them as a food, I suppose I would have to say that they are now a staple with me. Not incidentally, the pickle has also become a convenience food—

that is a term whose definition changes somewhat for the man without an icebox or a refrigerator. Pickles are convenient, of course, not because they are easy to fix, though they are that, requiring only the stabbing of a fork into a jar, but because they keep without spoiling. I am never nagged by the thought that my pickles might poison me, as my eggs may yet do, so I have naturally taken to eating lots of pickles. Ironically, I have eaten so many pickles that my palate threatens to go dead to the piquancy of dill-and-brine.

But it occurs to me now, as it never would have before, that my ancestors would probably miss the irony I see in my situation—it is one of those ironies permitted only to the modern viewpoint. My grandparents likely did not harbor the misconception, as I did for years, that pickling was first for taste and only incidentally for preserving. Now I eat pickles for the same reason they did and I grow jaded with pickles for the same reason they did, and even though I have not checked an encyclopedia to verify that I am right, I am sure now that I know the history of pickles and that this time I am reading that history right-side up.

In this rather unorthodox way I read into domestic history and write out my genealogy. Though my work is not bookish like the traditional genealogist's, though I have not been to the churches and courthouses, and even though I can still name you no names, I have found out my people because they must certainly have lived all or parts of their lives much as I am living now. Life at Nym suggests to me what the in-between times were to them, and I have a feel for the succession of their common days and common nights.

So what? someone says—or was about to. You are only poking about in a boneyard; you are merely an antiquarian, a hobbyist collecting antique experiences the way someone else would collect antique tools. What of your newfound knowledge is transferrable to the present century, the one to

which you must inevitably return? What good is all this,
except to gawk at with the mind's eye?

Once—last spring—such questions would have seemed to
me more telling than they do now. If I gawk, and I suppose I
do, I am not ashamed of it. Perhaps instead I am a little
proud. Mind is no different from muscle in this respect: Both
need movement to maintain their healthy elasticity. The
mind's eye, it turns out, *requires*—and this is part of the
mind's geometry—something to gawk at, though I would
prefer a less pejorative term than *gawk*, perhaps
contemplate, or if that is not neutral enough, then simply
think or *consider*. The healthy mind is compelled toward
newness and the unknown, and if you no longer believe that
some things are interesting in and of themselves, if you are
no longer interested in some things for no particular reason at
all—"curious," as we say—then you are crippled, like an
eagle with clipped wings who no longer soars for his food and
joy.

And I object to such carping questions for these reasons,
too: In addition to belying strangulated opinions about the
possibilities that exist under the sun, these impatient demands of the apologists for relevance are themselves irrelevant—and I would think that what follows would carry special
weight with them. Such pragmatists make a rash assumption
that is out of character with their usual timidity, that
assumption being that the useful can easily be distinguished
from the useless. Experience should suggest the contrary.
Sadly—a pragmatist would say—I have not done well in
making these distinctions. Once I compiled a list of books
that had had more than a passing influence on my life. One
might expect there to be a certain self-evident augustness to
the list of any serious reader—so at least I consider myself.
Imagine my surprise, then, at discovering that my own list
was tainted with too many oddities and was something less

than distinguished. What was actually astonishing, however, was my realization that if this list were to be a true one—and I thought seriously for a moment of falsifying it—it would have to include, of all things, a cookbook.

Who would have guessed? I remember buying the book out of an impulse no firmer than pale curiosity—very pale, as I recall it—but by slow degrees this book, along with one other that followed, turned me away from meat-and-potatoes cookery, and now when I use meat at all, it is mostly as a condiment, like the salt pork that is flavoring the beans. What had once been an irrelevant curiosity (as all curiosities are) has drastically altered my diet, which of all human habits is one of the least amenable to change. What was once vastly irrelevant is now highly relevant—three times each day. As I say, who would have guessed?

The instance of the cookbook is neither the exception nor the rule—my record at culling the relevant from the irrelevant is very spotty—and I am ready to admit that there is more to this winnowing process than simply tossing up for consideration a hodgepodge of possibilities and then expecting to separate them with the telling wind of my intellect or intuition. I have given up fortune telling and for the most part I hang back from judgment so that the future might have its say. For the most part. I am not always successful at biding my judgment; in fact, I have at times failed miserably at it by, for instance, peevishly damning entire bodies of knowledge in my profession as mere collections of academic graffiti that have attained respectability, perhaps even acclaim, because they happen to have been scribbled onto pages rather than walls. Of course that ornery judgment may eventually prove correct, but for the time being I counsel myself to define that word *relevant* generously and never to disparage any information that comes my way about the world. Ultimately, I am more interested in relevance than

that misnamed pragmatist who demands first and last, What's
it good for?—by which he really means, What's it good for
now? I meander amongst the obscurities, like the things my
grandparents knew, because I am curious about them, but
also because they might prove sometime to be—yes—useful.
When you ride the flux, it pays to be nimble.

Yet I think I can satisfy even the narrowest pragmatist's
demand that my antiquarian knowledge be directly useful to
me when I leave Nym in September to reenter my own time.
As it turns out, there is something in this experience that is
readily transferrable to the urbanized, regimented twentieth
century, something that I believe can improve our mass
existence. It is not the novelty of my domestic arrangements—which I have so much enjoyed—that I will be able to
take with me. Newness diminishes quickly, especially when
there is any physical labor involved. A sheet scrubs much like
a shirt, except that there are buttons to watch out for on the
shirt, and when you have washed the one you have really
washed the other, too, at least as far as the novelty of it goes.
Newness never lasts, and weeks ago I had worn out whatever
novelty there is in my domestic arrangements. So it is not the
novelty, nor is it even the actual learning of the task and the
addition of it to my body of skills that I can take with me and
that I value most: Strangely, ironically, it is the repetition of
the task once learned, the same repetition that we are told
feeds and eventually fattens boredom and drudgery, that I
prize most of all.

Machines have stolen away the repetition from us under
the guise of saving our labor. We suppose that we do not yet
have enough labor-saving appliances and machines to rid
ourselves—O, heavenly day!—of the last remnant of physical
drudgery. One more appliance will usher in a new age—a
device, say, whose specialty (and, incredible as this sounds,
whose only *possibility*) is to cook a hamburger in sixty

seconds flat, or another appliance that threatens to do the same thing to a hotdog in equal time. It has gone largely unnoticed that the problem of physical drudgery was solved some time ago and that now the problem for householders is that our labor-saving devices are saving too much of our labor. We have wandered from the golden mean. Without really intending it, we have absolved ourselves from contact with the physical world, and we hoard our labor and no longer extend our senses into the world as we once did. Without a corresponding expansion of spirit, we have become disembodied, and in our unnatural abstinence we deny our creaturehood and dangerously mortify the flesh. The world, I would say, is not enough with us, and it is hardly a sin to be of the world. Where else is there to be?

No machine saves my labor. I am my own machine, and hence my own man, and I am a believer in the primacy of the flesh. I would not want to be mistaken as a believer in the primacy of the crotch—they are not the same thing. The super-sensualists who sing the body electric by means of battery-powered dildos, life-sized dolls humanized with vinyl parts, and other aids to a cold or sagging libido constrict sensual experience, and I am in favor of expanding it. They are specialists where I am a generalist, and sometimes I wonder whether they have not been driven to their specialty because they are dead, or close to it, to every other sensuality but the most powerful and precious of them, and that their obsession is born of the fear that they will lose *that* one, too. Instead of constricting the varieties of sensual experience, perhaps they should expand them. When the flesh is weak, all the senses need restoring. Like muscles, senses can be strengthened through proper repetition, and just as the repetition can add a lost joy to our lives—the joy in our animality and not simply in our sexuality—it can also restore our lost sense of control over the in-between times.

Housewifery

Each day I saw, split, and stack firewood, and, like Henry Thoreau, I am twice warmed by it. But there is considerably more that can be said for cutting your own wood. There is the warmth, to be sure, but there is also the sound: the buzzing song of my saw as it transects the log in stately measures. There is the sight: freshly split balsam, a pure bright blond along the new plane left by the cleaving axe. There is the smell: the fragrance of cedar sawdust, rich as coffee, as the raker teeth sweep the tiny chips out of the saw-kerf where they drift to the forest floor. And there is the touch: as I work at the sawbuck, the feel of my own blooded muscles expanding, contracting, taut with action, with life, and at home in a task thoroughly known, like a good sled dog in the harness. Sometimes I saw for hours, for the pure joy of it, and I have more wood than I need—I am getting ahead of myself—enough to last me into the cool, sometimes wintry days of September. Though on some hot and humid afternoons I have found a momentary but fulfilling exhaustion in the sawing and splitting, I have not yet plumbed any drudgery in these tasks. Instead of avoiding it when I can, I value the repeated action, like the push and pull of the saw and the swing of the axe, and I seek it out. There is satisfaction, even joy, in such acts, and not in spite of the repetition but in large measure because of it. I think of the shining agates I searched for as a boy along the sand beaches of the Great Lakes. To the hunter who digs for them, they are semiprecious; once plain stones, they have been polished to a new and higher value by centuries of the ceaseless laving surf. Like those agates, my drab tasks as a householder are polished by repetition to a more perfect value, and in their transformation they have become semiprecious to me.

Though I could buy my bread in town, I much prefer to bake it myself. Bread is my staff of life—I eat nearly a pound of it a day—and so that I might always have fresh bread I never bake more than a pair of loaves at once. It is good wheat bread I bake, with something to it, not mere stuff, stuffing, like the white bread from the store that melts sadly in your mouth, as if you had wanted a communion wafer for your soul instead of food for your body. When I first begin to mix the dough it has the consistency of slough mud. How, I ask each time, can this gluey mess ever become palatable, even edible? As I add flour the dough stiffens, and I turn it out of the bowl and work it on the counter. With the heels of my hands hollowing the doughy mass, I turn the dough a quarter at a time, folding each edge in its turn into the hollow left by my hands. I work without hurry—that was the hardest part to learn—slowly turning, pressing, turning, pressing, adding flour as I go until the dough is ready for rising. Then I set the bowl of dough in the sun or on the railing in the loft, and mysteries, maybe miracles, are performed: Yeast grows and gluten forms, and when the mass is ready to be proofed into loaves, it is firm and glistening and twice its former size. The ball of dough is a thing alive, kneaded to life in my hands.

Forty minutes after the second rising I find dark jewels hidden in the blackness of the oven, and I can never wait for the rough-crusted loaves to cool. As soon as I have them out of their pans, I slice two slabs of the steaming bread from off a loaf-end and cut a fat wedge from the wheel of cheese. It is exquisite food, this smooth sharp cheese, as ripe and smoky yellow as a full moon floating on a snowfield, and this coarse bread, dark and sweetly flavored with molasses and honey, to which it is joined. Such food is exquisitely and especially fit for the man who made it, as it cannot help but be. Each piece of bread is seeded with the remembrance of my making it, which so educates, so refines and sharpens my palate that there can be no more discriminating taster of this food than myself.

Housewifery

Sometimes I half-expect—half-hope—that I will merge with the broad dough as I knead it in my hands or that I will become one with the saw as it does its work. I have read accounts by others who say that through repetition of word or act—and language begins to fail them here—they have merged, if only for a moment, into the One that is said to supersede or encompass or embody the Many. From some source unknown to me, I myself have received intimations that the One does in fact exist, but as yet I have had no vision to stand as my proof. Though I have not merged with the One, I count myself lucky to have at least lost track of myself amongst the Many. My menial tasks are self-effacing and mindless—mind-less in the high and most healthy sense of that term—because the doing of the task blanks the self-reflecting portion of my mind. For minutes, sometimes for hours, I am spared the sight of myself in that hall of mirrors which is the consciousness of my own consciousness. Too many of those images, as I have discovered, can paralyze mind and will, but in the doing of a task my most inward eye closes, mesmerized perhaps by the motion, and the rest of me is wholly captured in and by the pure and vital immediacy of the task at hand. Gone also in the midst of the repeated act is another dimension of mind, the knowledge of time that hangs like a scrim at the back of the mind and against which all our more conscious thoughts are projected. Too often that scrim devitalizes and trivializes the now. Yet in the midst of the repeated act I can be merely and supremely an object among objects, synthesized into my surroundings rather than analyzed out of them. The mind meets a quietus but not a dullness, and I stop seeing myself.

So I recommend housewifery, at least as I practice it, to anyone who grows weary, perhaps sick like Prufrock, at the sight of himself. Menial tasks, if they are not practiced to the point of absurdity, not only can restore and refresh the mind, to say nothing of the body, but they also can recapture our lost sense of control. We need to be prime movers, actors more than we are re-actors, to extend ourselves into the world rather than merely submitting, meekly or not, to its violations of us. But the proportion of actor and re-actor in modern life has been reversed. That is why it is important to me that no food engineer has designed into my bread some cancerous chemical intended to preserve it from the mold or to give it a homey taste. I provide the homey taste and a handmade texture myself, and I change both the taste and the texture according to my whim and the contents of my pantry. At one baking the bread may be heavy with raisins, at another spiced with cheese or sugared with sorghum syrup. On no two bakings is the bread quite the same, though it is always exactly the same in this one respect: It is always exactly as I would have it. Likewise, I know the history of the beans that are baking in the oven, and when they begin to ferment in a few days from lack of refrigeration, I will know that that strange effervescence is the action of yeast growing, which can be boiled away, and not some inert and unpronounceable ingredient come to kill me.

I would not make too much of this, lest no one believe me. To saw your own wood, which is unfortunately out of the question for most of us, or to bake bread or beans, will perhaps not transform the core of your private world, unless it leads you to the One that I suspect, but for the office worker trapped in towers of steel and glass for whom the flux is a ceaseless flow of paper, for the production worker who believes he may as well be strapped onto the assembly line as chained next to it, for any man who is only a cog in the wheels or a link in the chain of command, thoroughly and immediately dispensable, the kitchen is a fine place to begin one's rebellion against the disastrous proportions of contemporary life.

Housewifery

I am indulging in some highly constructive rebellion, and, because this summer I have acquired and fed—an interest in things antique, I've also naturally come to wonder what has happened to the gracious life that we now associate almost exclusively with the past. *Gracious* is a word not much used in our time, apparently because gracious living is extinct, having been killed off along with passenger pigeons and "ladies" by the turns that modern life has taken. As for my life at Nym, that would seem to be as far from gracious as any could be. It is primitive, some would say even crude. Right now, for instance, I am sitting at the kitchen table writing my mind on the backs of dog-eared scratch paper. The tabletop and my lap are littered with tiny threads of tobacco, the leavings of a chain of cigarettes I've rolled and smoked while sitting here. In a few minutes when the bread is out of the pan, I'll sit down to what easily passes with me as gourmet fare, a bowl of baked beans and a cheese sandwich, and my plate will probably be the breadboard, which is a foot-long section of scrap two-by-ten that I scrounged one day from beneath the cabin. If I need a napkin, the back of my hand is close by and will suffice—one is less fastidious living alone. As for my clothes, my pants might be taken as representative. They are a pair of paint-spattered khakis that at the moment have a spot of pitch on the backside, and I can feel myself stick to the chair whenever I shift my bones. As for what used to be called one's toilet, I have not shaved for a week—here shaving is a prelude to an Occasion, and my last Occasion was a town trip of some seven or eight days ago. And perhaps I can even smell myself.

So at first it will sound a little strange when I tell you that life at Nym is gracious—that, in fact, it is never more gracious than on mornings such as this one. Gracious living, I have concluded, does not depend on a fat portfolio of tax-free bonds or blue-chip stocks. Nor is it defined by any of the usual stereotypical, monied images like wing-backed leather chairs in front of library fireplaces, or frosted mint juleps sipped by ladies and gentlemen in white who repose on the verandah in the heat of the day. Nor do even good taste, elegance, ease, or luxury have much to do with the gracious life, except in an incidental way. They are neither synonymous with gracious living nor a necessity for it; instead, one might say they are only possibilities for gracious living.

My primitive manner of living is gracious because, for one thing, I am surrounded by the natural beauties, which are as tasteful as tasteful can be. But more important, there is a sense of proportion to my life, and it is this sense of proportion that is the prerequisite—and not simply a perquisite—of gracious living, and that distinguishes it from merely luxurious, indolent, or dissipated living. Life here is comprised of action and contemplation; it is balanced, as it were, between the two. Moreover, action and thought are not divorced from each other. Action naturally and gracefully shades into thought, as when I sat down this morning to wait for the dough to rise.

Sitting here at the table I have spent the morning inquiring into whether there is any significance, apart from the obvious practical necessities, in the menial tasks of my days at Nym. I could not account for the satisfaction and joy I found in such menial—and hence, almost by definition, meaningless—activities, and I suspected that there was more to my life than I was seeing, but whatever it was was a tangle, like a snag of fishline that needed unraveling. That I might sort out these things for myself, that I might know them rather than merely suspect them, I sat down here a few hours ago, not even sure exactly what it was I was about to do, and soon my mind was at work untangling thoughts with the tools that work best for me, pen and paper.

My morning's activity has been an instance of mind plying

matter. In our culture we would probably phrase that somewhat differently—"mind over matter," we might say. Before this morning I would have perfunctorily agreed with the general validity of that cracker-barrel aphorism, never having taken the time to work out its possible meanings, and I would also have agreed that the phrase is applicable to my morning. But I am aware of more of those meanings now, and I beg to differ with some of them. This morning's work tells me not only that you can have both mind and matter, but what is more, that you need both. Mind *and* matter is what I say—it seems to be a more inclusive truth and one that more accurately describes my morning.

I was unaware of this when I sat down this morning, and I wrote that things would soon be complete—I meant only taking the bread from the oven, and I had only the vaguest hint at first of the other ways in which things can be brought to completion. I now see a completion of greater significance, the dovetailing of thought and act, and I now know that the morning will come to fullness not when I open the oven door but as I write the last of these words.

THE CLOCK

Chapter Six

Not that the hours before high noon are the best to fish the narrows running into Black Bay. Dusk is best, but I was there anyway this morning, my patience and my taste for angling having been broadened this summer. Sometimes they are biting, sometimes not, but the fishing is always good in the narrows. Dropping my line in that watery byway on such days as today is too great a temptation to resist, and I was anchored in the channel this morning as much to laze in the shadows cast by the pines that hover over the water as I was there to catch fish. If I caught one I would come away with a bonus; if not, no matter. The glories of the morning being sufficient unto themselves, I could tolerate, and have before, the ignominy of canned tuna for my supper.

Last night a thunderstorm hurried through making everything new again. The wind and rain swept the earth clean, and colors today were bolder and more solid, shapes sharper, the air storm-distilled. As I fished in the bright wake of the storm, wind-devils played out on the main body of the lake, prickling here and there the flat water. From my vantage point back in the channel, the ripples of water showed themselves as ripples of light, which looked like sunlight sharping off the scales of some great fish as it broke the surface again and again.

As I drifted in and out amongst the shadows, the only sound was the whir of my line paying out with each cast and the neat *punkt* of the lure as it hit the water. Casting-and-reeling, casting-and-reeling, I fell sway to the rhythm of my morning's occupation, and my thoughts had begun to drift as aimlessly as the boat when I was drawn from my incipient reverie by a thud. It was a sound I had heard hundreds of times: people. In the age of aluminum, that telltale thud is more often than not the first sign of people approaching. The emblem of the lazy or weak or inexperienced, the sound is the by-product of a canoe paddle being pried against an aluminum gunwale to increase the leverage, and not incidentally the power, of the stroke. At odd intervals the familiar sound repeated itself, each time a bit louder and more distinct than the last, and in a few minutes a canoe hugging the shore rounded the bend heading toward me in the narrows.

A man and a young teenaged boy, father and son I figured, were paddling toward me. When they were in speaking range, I waved because it is an insult not to acknowledge your own kind, especially when they make their appearance but rarely. The man, who was paddling stern, waved back and asked how the fishing was. Nothing yet, I had to tell him. Not having spoken to anyone for over a week, I was ready for talk, isolation increasing the desire to be sociable and mannerly, and the man must have sensed that they would not be unwelcome intruders on my solitude. When they were within easy conversational range the man drew up his paddle and the boy did likewise. While we made the obligatory comments on the fine weather, the man reached forward to a Duluth pack resting against the stern thwart and retrieved a pack of Camels that was tucked under the flap and offered me one of his American-made ready-rolls. They were from Chicago, the man said, and this was the first day of a two-week canoe trip into the Quetico. When I told him that I lived in a cabin on the lake, they both began to ask questions about the proposed trip their outfitter had described to them and traced on their map. The boy, a spectacled tube of nerves and bones, asked in a squeaky-new bass voice if any of the lakes on their route were sure bets for big fish, and I made some suggestions, which he circled on the map. For his part, the man, whose bulk in middle age had begun to shift centerward, was interested in my opinion on the difficulty of the trip, and I concurred with the outfitter's claim that for a two-week trip theirs seemed easy to middling. My opinion seemed to please the man, though it had no discernible effect on the boy, who sat fidgeting in the bow seat, his paddle resting across his knees but gripped and ready for action.

Saying they'd best be moving along, the man dropped his spent cigarette butt into the water and watched it soak up, then gripped his paddle and made ready to move out. But before the paddle could cut the water on the first stroke, the man stopped to ask one more question. In a tone that was at once quizzical and apologetic, as if he were asking an uncommonly large favor of a stranger, he said: "Say, you wouldn't know what time it is?" He pointed to his wristwatch and explained that it was an old one he saved for vacations. He had forgotten to set it when he strapped it on this morning.

As it happened, I didn't know the time, but I told him that if I had to guess, I'd say it was—and then I made some private calculations—eleven o'clock. The two of them then decided it would be a good idea to put forward guesses of their own, which were apparently based on interpolations as private as mine, and because three heads are better than one, we decided to average the answers. It was 11:15 A.M. Saying to no one in particular that this was better than nothing, the man carefully set his watch. While he was winding the watch stem the boy suddenly erupted with exasperation, or perhaps inspiration, it was hard to say. "Who *cares*," he wanted to know. The words were as much declaration as question, and, it being moot whether any answer was required or expected, none was forthcoming. The watch set and wound, they again took up their paddles and we said our goodbys and wished each other good fishing and good weather. Thus armed with the democratically computed time, the two of them paddled off into the wilderness.

The thud resumed its uneven cadence, and while I watched them inch out of sight into Black Bay, I wondered about the man's final question, What time is it? I was indifferent to the accuracy of our composite answer, curious instead about the question generally considered and about those who ask the question. Maybe I had met this man before in the Quetico and he had asked me the time then, too, and if I had not met him before I had encountered others like him, the most memorable of whom is the man I saw on Conmee Lake a few years ago when I was guiding. Thirty miles from the nearest road and probably another ten or twenty from the nearest clock, the man paddled two miles down the lake to find out whether anyone in my crew knew the answer to one vital and anxiously asked question: What time is it? We could have sold him the time, I'm sure, and so added a new twist to Poor Richard's wisdom that time is money. When someone amongst us produced a watch, the man visibly relaxed, and the viscera-deep tension, which apparently affected both mind and muscle, instantaneously dissipated as the answer was read off. When he turned about to paddle back to his

The Clock

camp, the man left in a state of quiet euphoria similar to the one seen in a nicotine addict who has just had his first smoke in three days. If you had not known that it was a three-digit number that had produced such beatific calm, you could have been fooled into thinking the man had encountered that peace which is said to pass all understanding. And it must have been a peace of sorts since the time was certainly as priceless as a cigarette, but, presumably, his peace was of short duration since he told us before departing that no one in his party had thought to bring a watch.

Not everyone would be willing to paddle across a lake to beg for the time, and this time junkie's habit was obviously at an advanced stage. Yet if there is a more commonly asked question than What time is it?, I can't think of what it is. Though the answer keeps changing, one might be excused for classifying it with the Enduring Questions simply on the basis of the number of times we ask it of ourselves and others. It is likely that What time is it? was the first thing you asked yourself when you woke this morning—that is, unless you had already made arrangements with a rasping alarm clock to tell you even before you had a chance to ask; it is equally as likely that What time is it? was the last thing you asked yourself last night before deciding to go to bed—because it was "time," of course. There can be no doubt that it is exceedingly important for us to know what time it is. Learning to read the clock, like learning personal cleanliness, is a mandatory part of our socialization. Later we are taught to accept the value of clock time as we do the value of a federal reserve note, and society functions most smoothly when we simply accept both as a part of the given. It is a little subversive to inquire too closely into the ultimate value of either of them, and we accept the common time with the common currency because the orderly functioning of society depends on our mutual agreement to arrange that our bodies, goods, and services be in precisely described spots at precisely described times.

It may be hair-splitting, but certainly not idle hair-splitting, to note the differences between the minutes, and life can be uncertain for those who fail at it. Once I clerked in an office where one of my fellow workers did not parse the minutes as closely as the rest of us, and as a result his workday coincided only haphazardly with everyone else's. Tardiness, of course, is common enough. What distinguished this individual from the textbook laggard is that he did not seem to make those mental arrangements which allowed him to "forget" the time. His ignorance, as far as I could tell, was pure, unsullied by rebelliousness or any other ulterior motive. As one might suppose, such colossal indifference to the minutes was a constant irritation to our employer, who could not even count on the man's being late, and our supervisor no more understood this breach of social and business etiquette than he would have understood someone who persisted in spitting on the floor. For that matter, the office laggard was equally strange to the rest of us, and he had only to walk out the door five minutes early to remind us anew of his irresponsibility or foolhardiness or bravery or indifference, as the case might be, but whatever we as individuals thought of him, there was common agreement that he was odd. Time is money, as Poor Richard said it was, and I sometimes wonder whether Franklin ever guessed at the zeal with which we would drive the metaphor from his aphorism. Those who fail, as our office laggard did, to recognize the rightness of Poor Richard's equation blaspheme the social order or at the least are guilty of an intolerable myopia. No matter the degree of the transgression, the practical result is often the same, and we were all surprised that this singular fellow was not fired sooner than he was.

The Clock

But most of us are well adjusted and submit with facile ease to the regimentation of the clock. It is not hard to see why. Men have always been much interested in knowing what time it is, and we have been measuring the hour for 5500 years, ever since the Egyptians fashioned the first crude timekeeping device, which was nothing more than a vertical stick whose shadow marked off the divisions of the day. The history of horology is largely the history of building ever more regular and reliable clocks and watches, and the most recent benefit of the collective genius, the atomic clock, tells time by means of measuring the electromagnetic frequency in the very particles that compose matter. The atomic clock is miraculously accurate—if in the present age *miraculous* is ever merited, this would seem to be an instance—to within one second every 100 centuries.

Even more than these technological and scientific feats, it is the public's quick and glad acceptance of them, especially during the last hundred years, that tells the tale of our fascination with time. A hundred years ago if a man owned a watch it was most likely a pocket watch. About the turn of the century people began to discover the fatal flaw of the pocket watch, which was that it was so poorly designed that it required its own pocket and had to be taken out and put away, and in some cases even opened and closed, all to find out something as simple and elementary as the correct time.

It was the wristwatch that unblinded us to the deficiencies of the pocket watch. The design of the wristwatch was obviously superior since it permitted the wearer to check the time with a deftly synchronized flick of the wrist and dart of the eye. Further, it required no special pockets or clothing, which meant that it could be worn even to bed. No longer did one need to go through the silly and rather irritating labor of fumbling with a watch fob, following it to its special pocket, lifting the watch out, uncapping the face, holding it

109

forward at a visually comfortable distance, reading the hands, and then recapping the watch and returning it to its pocket. With a wristwatch the time became available automatically, as it were, and though there were some feeble objections about the fashionableness of the new watches, among them the curious idea that it was effeminate to wear a watch but not to carry one, the wristwatch quickly supplanted the pocket watch. Such progressive efficiency does not go unnoticed or unrewarded, and as a result the wristwatch has never suffered the usual periodic eclipses in popularity that other fashions like wide ties and button-down collars are prone to. A wristwatch today is really not an accessory to fashion at all, like stickpins or earrings. It is more like a set of dentures.

Mass production and the near total acceptance of the wristwatch have tied us tightly to clock time. Like the automobile, the wristwatch created—insinuated is perhaps a better word—a need for itself. Men are passionate measurers of everything, seen or unseen, and when the correct time is no longer buried in a pocket but is in constant full view at the end of your arm, of course you note the time more often. It never becomes necessary to check the time two, three, four, five, six times an hour until the minute is as freely, as automatically, available as it is to the owner of a wristwatch. Such easy availability not only points the way toward necessity, it paves the way, too, and at present the wristwatch is what might be called a gratuitous necessity. That is, it is not yet a true necessity in the way that a car is said to be for people living in Los Angeles, but it cannot be doubted that when you check the time as often as we do, it makes eminently good sense to check it on a wristwatch.

Advances made in the wristwatch suggest that it is becoming less gratuitous and more an outright necessity. Luminous dials were added for those in the dark, constant improvements are being made in its accuracy, and an ingenious fail-safe device has been introduced on most models because the constant availability of the correct time has assumed such importance that we feel uncomfortable subjecting its keeping to the frailties of human memory. That latest advance, the digital-faced watch that is powered by a revolutionary quartz crystal, further advances the utility of the wristwatch because it resurrects the sole advantage of the pocket watch, which was its easy readability, and combines that readability with an accuracy never before achieved in a cheap, mass-produced watch. Never again need anyone mistake 9:22 for 9:23, and, judging from the increasing numbers of the new watches making their appearance, it is a mistake fewer and fewer of us are willing to make. No doubt that fellow on Conmee Lake, wherever he is now, appreciates enough this fortunate combination of easy readability and supreme accuracy to have purchased a quartz watch. And when the rest of us have purchased ours, he will probably own one of the new atomic watches, or its equivalent, which is perhaps now in some early stage of development in the labs of a great public corporation whose eye looks unblinkingly for the main chance. This futuristic chronometer will lure the prospective purchaser by offering him the soundest assurance yet that if he cannot be in tune with the universe, he can at least be in sync with it.

So it is that we submit to the domination of the clock. We submit, that is, except during those two weeks of vacation each year when our habit of timekeeping is no longer viewed as admirable or necessary but as irritating, even pernicious. There may be justice in clock time, but there is no mercy in it, and during those fourteen days at the end of twelve long months, it is our earned right as laborers to slip the traces which bind us to clock time in favor of finding or establishing a private sense of time that does not chafe. For a man on vacation there would scem little reason for knowing, and much reason for not knowing, the time. But in practice what often happens is that we remain tied to the clock, that knot being one of Gordian difficulty, and we simply give ourselves a little more line by changing anchors from the minute to the hour hand. If by chance or design we should cleave the knot which binds us, the freedom gained is often not as appreciated as one might expect, as I was reminded by the man in the narrows this morning. Maybe he asked me the time because he remembered a past vacation when he had made the mistake of leaving his watch at home and then found out that he had more than a pragmatic or dispassionate interest in knowing the time. He may even have conscientiously attempted to avoid knowing the time, only to make the sour discovery that the time was paradoxically present through its very absence.

Being more perfectly socialized than his adolescent son, I can sympathize with the man's itch to know the time. I have had the itch myself. For several years now I have carried a pocket watch, not as a badge of wisdom or because I am nostalgia-bitten, but as a dose of preventative medicine to allay that most socially benign body tic, the flick of the wrist, which had begun to deliver up the time just a little too automatically for me. When I arrived at Nym in June it was my intention to retire even this innocuous timepiece to the oblivion of the dresser drawer. My ties with town would be elastic enough, I thought, that there was no reason I should lock myself into the rigid rhythm of the common time.

But the plan to put away the watch was delayed. On the bookshelf I found a wind-up alarm clock that I didn't remember seeing before. Out of curiosity I wound it to see if it ran. It did. Motivated again by what I regarded as simple curiosity, I decided to postpone for a while giving up my

pocket watch so that I might use it to find out how accurate
the alarm clock was. By the time I had found out the clock
was reasonably accurate, I had grown used to the long and
lazy meter the clock marked out, and I had become somewhat fond in that short time of such a restful sound. I also
regarded the tick as a gently whispered exhortation reminding me, in case I should forget, that Nym was schedule-free.
No clock at all, of course, would have been the best
expression of that sentiment, and this fact was not lost on me;
nevertheless, I was content to settle for the penultimate
expression of my belief because, as I told myself, I rather
liked the soothing measures the clock tapped out.

This was no ordinary clock, or at least no ordinarily
conceived of clock. I thought of it more as a music box than a
clock, an instrument that meted out its tune for me day and
night. Yet I knew it was only a short step from regarding that
music, if I remembered to regard it at all, as merely a by-
product of that regulatory information that a clock provides. I
wanted no strict regulator where none was needed, and
though I got some small pleasure from the clock's presence, I
suspected that it could become omnipresent, especially since
the room where it sits is most often empty of any sound save
the tick of the clock. Such a suspicion seemed good enough
reason to turn the clock's face to the wall. Instead, I
compromised: I would wind the clock and keep its face in full
view, but I would guard against regulating my life by the
clock, or even assuming that it had any but a kind of
gratuitous information to offer me.

For a while I balanced on that thin edge of dispassionate
interest, and I followed the clock with the same weak
curiosity that a college student might follow for a class
assignment the daily fluctuations of a randomly chosen
common stock. I ate when my stomach growled and slept
when I got tired, and if in those first days of my saurian

lethargy I did not eat or sleep on my former civilized schedule, the change was only temporary, I thought, and when I chanced to look at the clock, I dutifully reminded myself that the clock meant no more than if it had been set to London or Peking time.

But it is a compromising position to be both observer and observed, and eventually I lost my balance on that cultivated edge of disinterested interest. I became too much of a curiosity to myself. Instead of returning naturally to my former schedule, I began to drift further and further from it, and my three daily meals—on those days when I ate three meals—began to bunch themselves closer together at the far end of the day, which occasioned astonishment first, then apprehension. Though I had in the past lived comfortably in this country for weeks at a time without a watch, I began to see that my own biological clock was as yet virtually untested because I had never lived alone. There had always been at least one companion against whom I could check, however unconsciously, whatever small warps had begun to make their appearance in my own interior sense of time. Alone, I could not tell if that sense of time had begun to stretch and find its natural shape, in the manner of a butterfly at last free of the chrysalis, or if my sense of time were simply running completely amok.

Though I had sworn off the clock as my regulator, I lacked the confidence in my untested private sense of time, which through disuse might have withered, and as I strayed further and further from the common time, the clock became more and more fascinating—as did my own interest in the clock, which by then was undeniable. Apparently I was regarding the clock as something more than an oil can that dispenses lubricant to fine-tune the social machinery. Even though I seldom had any desire to check the clock more than once or twice a day, I could not deny the curious relief that invariably

came in discovering the hour and minute. There was always
the question : Would I, or would I not, be surprised by what
the hands had to say? It was as if I expected the clock to
verify something for me or to correct and reset the angle of
my mental movement. The clock was like an astrolabe which
was to provide me a fix on my time, my place, in the flux of
my own life. My assumption—indeed, my wish—seemed to
be that the clock would reify, somewhat in the manner of
Plato's allegory of the cave, an absolute: Time.

It was the Newtonian time that the clock was supposed to
measure off, that "absolute, true, and mathematical time
which of itself, and from its own nature, flows equably
without relation to anything external." Einstein and twen-
tieth-century physics notwithstanding, I am still conducting
my everyday business in the world of Euclid and Newton, as
I believe others are also. As yet there is no room in our
minds, except as fable, for something as exotic as space-time.
No one, and I think this includes students of higher physics,
carries out the garbage in, or through, space-time. Time, we
hold, is an entity unto itself, linear, uniform, absolute: linear,
because time's arrow travels in one direction only, toward the
future; uniform, because each hour, each minute, each
second and picosecond is standardized, its length never
varying in theory and varying in practice only because of our
incapacity to construct the perfect tool of measurement;
absolute, because time's arrow is irreversible, because it is
the irresistible force which never meets the immovable
object, because it is not a building block of our world but a
prerequisite to it.

Is Time each of these things, or any of them? To ask is to
be lured off, as I was, into the weedy waters of Philosophy. I
will be short about it and not strain credulity by announcing
that I have discovered what Time is or how to accommodate
men to its passage (or, if you like, our passage through it or

through the illusion of it). We seem not to have the faculties to contemplate such questions directly, and my mind was staggered like eyes that look too long at the sun. All I got for the pleasures and pains of my meditation was a kind of intellectual vertigo. Having nothing to replace it with, I have no objections to the currently respectable Western prejudice that Time is linear, uniform, and absolute. This view is still respectable with me, too.

Less respectable with me are the clocks that we wind to tell us the Time, and I blush to think of the seerlike labors I have demanded as a matter of course from a simple collection of springs and gears that can be had in any five-and-dime. Besides being a mundane tool to mark off the purely pragmatic workaday time, the clock is also a curious icon of our society. Like a Buddhist prayerwheel, it is an earthly tool performing an unearthly task: The clock's spiritual function is to objectify our private sense of the passage of Time. We ask too much of the clock. What the clock really measures, of course, is not Time but only one kind of time—specifically, mean solar time, a subtime of universal time, which is based on the rotation of Earth on its axis. Somewhere most of us have discovered, and then forgotten, that in addition to universal time there are two more kinds of time, ephemeris and atomic, and that these, too, are based on natural occurrences—respectively, the revolution of Earth about the sun, and the frequency of electromagnetic waves. What is even more easily forgotten—perhaps because it is so convenient to forget this—is that none of these natural events bears any necessary relationship to the others. If the solar system is a clock, then it presents for our edification several faces. None of them, not even the extraordinarily accurate atomic clock, is preferred over another except as a matter of convenience. It is, for example, convenient to measure duration, but not the instant, according to atomic time.

The Clock

Because it is now convenient, mean solar time is followed for civil purposes, though before technology rendered the sun dial obsolete, it was convenient to follow apparent solar time. Thus, the man I met this morning in the narrows need not have felt the least bit sheepish about setting his watch to our arbitrarily chosen time. As it turns out, democratically computed time is not only better than nothing, it is as good as anything.

But wait. That is flippant and thus unsatisfactory. In practice we are not so indiscriminating, so democratic, in our judgments on matters of importance. There is something insubstantial and ephemeral about the merely relative; it is inherently unsafe, like an ice floe, not the sort of thing one wants to rely on to plot one's position. The absolute is preferred. It is nothing if not substantial, safe as safe can be, and comfortable to boot. So, partly out of hope, with this hope fed by our long habit of clocks and watches, we blur the two, mean solar time and Time, and think of them as one.

Or want to think of them as one. But Heaven and Earth have not yet met, and clock time and Time seem to run at different rates. Spiritually considered, the track of the hands seems not so much wrong about the Time as irrelevant to it. But we are men of uncommon belief and we are believers anyway. Like the flatlanders of medieval days who wondered at the illusion of ships seeming to sink off the horizon into the sea, we find it strange how the clock and calendar so lamely mark the passage of Time. The mystery is disturbing but nevertheless an afterthought with us, and as such too slight to eat away at our assumption. Despite such broad hints that Time and mean solar time ought not to be confused, we persist in our great expectations of the clock, and this super-legitimacy that we confer upon the clock accounts for my own too-keen interest in the clock on the shelf just as it explains the unspoken embarrassment of the man in the narrows.

117

Keeping the time amounts to a religion with us, and in this instance, at least, the faith comes easy because religion is a community as well as an individual endeavor, and we are all sustained by a particularly strong community of believers. But the longer I am at Nym and apart from society, the less easy is the faith, which is probably why I am now able to separate the clock's spiritual from its earthly functions and more or less to ignore its message.

The clock is of no practical consequence to me. Simply put, this is a one man/one dog society. There is no person or institution to which I must, or even can, adjust, except once every week or so when I go in to town. Merchants do business during the hours of daylight, and for my purposes it is sufficient to know only the difference between day and night, a calculation that does not require a timepiece. Living alone has stripped the clock of its social utility, and even the most obtuse individual can believe in that utility for only so long before it begins to collapse of its own absurd weight, looking in its wreckage faintly ridiculous, like a pricked, wrinkled balloon.

Further, I discovered that my alarm over my atrophied sense of time was premature. Despite years of forced dormancy, my own biological clock is alive and healthy, serving effectively as my regulator and superimposing a more or less consistent shape to my days. More or less. My internal clock is by no means as regular as the mechanical variety, but it is enough of a regulator, all the regulator I need or care to have, allowing me, for instance, wide-eyed nights now and then when I read for hours by the light of the lamp and then walk through the blackest morning to the Toe to watch the stars or, if I'm particularly lucky, to gaze hang-jawed at curtains of light shimmering in the great vault of the northern sky. My regulator is not the clock, which is only an inaccurate transcription of the sun, but the sun itself, or if not the sun,

The Clock

then the wind and the roll of the waves, which if they sweep in with enough force leave me locked to the land. This is a very localized time zone, different because of the direction of the wind and the angle of the sun from even that time zone that prevails on the south shore across the bay. Wind, water, and sun are my external regulators, and I must synchronize my comings and goings to the natural elements, which can overpower me, and sometimes do, leaving me windbound for two and three days at a time.

I have supplanted the clock with other means more accurate and useful, and weeks ago I put away my pocket watch in the dresser drawer where it lies now, stopped. But I have not given up the clock. I still keep it wound and face-forward on the shelf. This moment I can hear it ticking away, forming the backdrop of my fountain pen etching its way across the paper. In a few minutes it will be seven "of the clock," as the the saying once was.

I regard that information differently now. After I have looked at the clock, I am more likely to be suspicious that I have just covertly asked it to bear false witness and tell me the Time that I might resynchronize myself to the pulse of the All. With my suspicion, which is also knowledge, I am able to muster enough clarity of mind to scoff at the answer. If the clock is a barren image of Time, so be it. There are better images: a journal volume bound in blue, lean or fat according to its time; on a nearby island a foot-high balsam that has sprouted so solidly and strongly from the flat rotting top of a sawn pine stump; a band of gold ringing my mother's hand, the gold now worn by generations to the frailness of the fingers it has circled; and—this very day—a maple leaf already eaten at its edges with red. These are better images, if not to dissolve some of the mystery of Time, then at least to move me closer to it, and it is not the clock but such images as these that serve.

Yet I still wind the clock. Who *cares*, the boy whined this morning. His father for one; I for another. The clock does serve in its way, otherwise I would not take it down from its shelf each night to wind it, nor would I ever hear its meter. But the clock is more than music, and I think I would wind it even if it had neither hands nor sound, and even though it is not now my external regulator or an occult tool that I use to give me a bead on the Absolute. My expectations of it are more reasonable. The clock links me, not to the universe at large but to the everyday world of men, and the clock is a remembrance that I am a man amongst men, though momentarily apart from them. I continue to wind the clock precisely because it records time in other places than Nym. Like ants and bees, we are social creatures who live in colonies, and the solitary life is laced with some peril. It is possible in living alone to become too much yourself, yourself distilled. That is a kind of drunkenness which in this country is called bush fever, and though it is hard to tell, I believe I have felt at times that peril sidling up to me. Maybe I have descended to superstition, but the clock, this symbol of our society, might be the amulet I may want to ward off mental fevers. The clock stands and waits.

As for the man and the boy, they have each other to prevent them from becoming too much themselves, if such is even possible in two weeks. I hope that they are camped on Pickerel Lake tonight where they wanted to be and are not pulled up into the bush on the edge of one of the potholes between here and there, nursing their first-day tiredness and cursing the steep hills and greased mud of the portages. But more than that, I hope neither one of them knows what time it is. That hope seems reasonable in the boy's case, much less so in the man's, unless he enjoyed the good fortune of losing or breaking his watch. If he was prevented by ill luck from doing so, I wish him better luck in the next few days while

The Clock

there is still some chance he can wean himself from the common time and enjoy a special freedom for a while. If a broken or lost watch is not in his future, then I take back my wish that they are camped comfortably and exchange it for a curse that they will meet with some benign disaster of the sort that makes a good story once it has passed. A misfortune can marvelously concentrate one's attention on the utter solidity of the hereness and nowness in the here and now, and the self-pitying misery that grows like a weed out of such moments can be so consuming as to betray the unimportance, even the folly, of everything, time and clocks included, which does not immediately ease that misery.

So, knowing there can be some ultimate profit in it, I wish upon them some small but healthy travail—their tent, say, pitched in too pronounced a hollow before the deluge. If that wish is excessively malevolent or mean-spirited, then it is only appropriate that someone as hard of heart as I should have to dine tonight on canned tuna, and not on the northern I fished for.

VOICES

Chapter Seven

Nothing satisfies. It is September, the best and worst of months. But now it is the worst, and if one of the float planes on fire patrol should by chance land out front, I would slam the door behind me and run down the hill out onto the Toe, waving all the while for the pilot to carry me up and away from this place. The wind has been blowing for the last four days. One phalanx of waves after another marches from east to west, creating a mighty east-flowing river where there was once a lake. The jackpine bend and sway in the wind like stalks of grain whipped by a prairie wind, and I must listen to the creaks and groans of their agonized contortions. How, I wonder, can they hold, hour after hour, year after year? But of course many of them do not.

I do not hold. For the last four days I have been trapped here on this spit of rock, windbound. The wind screams down the lake and through the trees, and there is nothing to do but read and eat and sleep and hide from the wind. But I have slept twelve hours of the last twenty-four, my stomach is sodden, stuffed with almost a whole tin of bran muffins, and I have finished my book and am too restless or too listless—I cannot tell which—to begin another. I am intolerable to myself. Bored stiff.

Zip, my companion, scratches lightly on the screen door, so I go to let her in. She is a liver-and-white brittany spaniel with a misshapen head. Had she been bred for show, Zip would have been put out of her breeder's misery long ago because of her Neanderthal brow, which sometimes gives her a vaguely stupid air. To her credit, though, the stupidity is fanciful rather than factual. Like any good all-around dog, Zip is schizophrenic. In the woods she is a proud hunter, and when she is snorting or pawing into some cranny or patch of brush, I can sometimes see—if I am close enough—an old and fierce light burning in the deeps of her eyes. It is the ancient animal fire, and in its presence I feel a like but paler fire flame in me, yet at the same time I am glad not to be the object of such sure and fearsome hunting. When Zip is in the cabin her smooth velvet eyes have lost all traces of their former fire, and she is civil and polite, even deferential. When she wants to come in, her scratch on the screen—it is really more like a caress—is unfailingly polite, just loud enough for me to hear her. She never snaps food from my fingers but always takes it neatly and gently, as if her teeth were razors. As for her loyalty—do I need to say this?—it is above reproach. She is faithful to the last degree. When I round the last island on my way back from town, she has already heard the drone of the outboard, and in the distance I see a tatter of white dancing in excitement on the Toe. Today is one of the few days Zip has gone off by herself for any length of time. She has been gone for four or five hours— perhaps I am intolerable to her, too.

I open the door her body-width and give a low quick whistle—her signal: in she scoots, happy—no, delirious—to see me. By way of greeting I give her ribs a couple of brisk

rubs and, running the words together, I growl excitedly,
"Where the hell ya been?" I can't remember the last time I
spoke, maybe yesterday, maybe the day before. My voice
sounds much louder than it should—or maybe than it really
is—and strange, somehow, in a way I can't define. I wonder
if through disuse I am abandoning my voice and must earn it
back. Squatter's rights on that, too.

"Where the hell ya been, huh!" I growl again, for
practice—and besides, it's something to do. In the last weeks
this tease has become something of a ritual with us. Zip is
calm now, sitting next to the table a few feet from me, and we
are looking at each other. "Where the hell ya been, huh!!" I
demand, my mock excitement even greater. She doesn't
know what to do. Her ears peel back on that sloping brow;
puzzled, she grins stupidly. I ask her again. This time her
eyes begin to flutter in a familiar nervous tic, and then they
almost close. She is blushing. So I ask her again: "Hey, you
old dog, where ya been, huh? Huh!" Zip is beside herself
wondering what it is that she is supposed to do. Maybe she
thinks I'm addle-pated; maybe I think so, too. What is certain
is that she's begging me to stop this teasing—the game has
gone on much longer than usual. Out of guilt I relent—a
little—and walk toward her. She turns belly-up like a dead
fish and I push her away from me. She creeps back like the
slave she is and we rassle around on the floor for a while to
make up, and Zip forgives me. Much sooner, I know, than I
would have forgiven her.

But after that there is nothing to do. Zip moseys off to the
alcove for a snooze, and I hear her arranging her rug in
proper disarray. She is curling herself into a donut, and then
I hear her sigh contentedly. She will be asleep—blissfully out
of her mind—in fifteen seconds. And here am I—wide-eyed
and envious.

So I pull on my wool jacket and windbreaker—again—set

my stocking cap at a square and determined angle, head out the door into the wind, and walk down to the Toe to see whether the wind has let up a little—just enough to take some of the risk out of crossing to the public landing so that I can escape to town for the rest of the afternoon. Shoulders hunched, elbows stiff and hugging my sides, my fists jammed deep into my pants pockets, I survey the unchanging scene. In the choppy gray water around the Toe, waves lick up at my feet, threatening to soak my mocassins. I am here to read weather sign so I look to the west. Toward town. I cock my head like a dog to fine-tune my ear, and I listen hard; this time I *really listen*. I read the sign with every sense, every pore and hair on my body. Eyes asquint and brow set in thoughtful pose, I detect—I think I detect—a lull. Then I wait a moment, I recheck, just to be sure. Yes . . . yes, the sky is beginning to lighten ever so slightly, I think I can see that, and there is a lull in the wind, that I can hear for sure. The waves a half-mile out are less surflike than they were an hour ago, the troughs not as wide and deep, and the whitecaps are definitely smaller and fewer. These are omens, as they cannot help but be, portents of things to come—and then I know with an assurance that I have seldom felt about anything that at last I am seeing the beginning of the end. Suddenly I am overflowing with happiness and gratitude and goodwill toward all things—everything is so sweet—so *right!*—with the world! I'll be in town in an hour!

As I am bailing out the boat I come to my senses. The lie was not big enough and my fragile exultation cracks, then splits wide open. I fancied that I, a modern man, was reading sign as if they were dials on an instrument panel. But I have been divining the weather like a priest his animal entrails. Or like a patient his inkblots. I know that by keeping to the leeward side of the islands I could weave this pitifully shallow and unseaworthy boat to within sight of the landing; I also

126

know—even though I tried my damnedest not to know this—
that if the weather howls here, it is nothing to the wall of
wind and surf that will slam into me as I round the last island
and head into the final few miles of open water. I am no
longer an innocent in such matters, and I have lost the
innocent's blithe courage and relish for such excitements. My
judgment gets the better of me and I decide, angrily, to stay
home.

So I climb a tree to scare myself—even if I am still captive
here, at least I can drive away this listless restlessness. My
choice is a virgin white pine spiked into the base of the Toe.
Hugging the pine like a bear, I claw and shinny my way up a
few inches to the first stob and then pull myself into the
lower branches. And climb. The wind-ripped branches are
dry and brittle, and as I gingerly test the dead ones I imagine
each of them shattering like glass. But none of them do, and
when I am thirty feet into the air, high enough to be riding
the tree in the wind, I stop and look down at the boat moored
a hundred feet or so beneath me. The sight of the toy boat
bobbing stupidly far below me quickens my blood and I hug
the tree for safety's sake: In that one moment I find all the
fear I climbed for.

Once I am a little used to my position, I savor the chaos of
wind and height. I am a boy riding a birch, a sailor out on a
yardarm, a fly riding the tip of a cracking whip, King Lear
raging on a storm-dark heath. I try out the part of Lear for
size and swear something defiant into the wind. For safety's
sake—my madness is still tentative—I am careful not to
loosen my grip so I can shake my fists while I shout. The
blasphemy helps, but it would be considerably more satisfying if thoughts of Lear had not intruded to compromise my
spontaneity. Today I am burdened even by what I have read.

The wind is tearing through the treetop ten or fifteen feet
above me, and the tree and I are cheek to cheek. As high as I

care to climb, I crane my neck to see out from the tree. If I could only just *see* out of here—south across the white-flecked grayness into the next bay, maybe, or if not that far, then at least into a tiny slough a few hundred yards up the shore. I climb for the prize, up two branches, then up one more. My knuckles are white, my knees feel as if they could buckle any second as I rock back and forth in the branches, but this is important, so I climb one more rung anyway.

To see nothing. There is no prize in this tree. This pine is not tall enough, or it could be that my fear or good judgment is taller than the tree. Whatever it is, I climb back down, a failure. As if I need reminding, a branch breaks and I slip, adding a kind of insult to the injury of my failure. When I reach the too-solid earth, the wind there is miserably old, blowing with the same dull battering force.

Could I go for a walk in the woods to escape this trap, pack a lunch—maybe a supper, too—and walk off this captivity? No. The answer comes flat and quick. I have tried escaping into the bush during other blows when I was bound to the cabin. The strong woods are close, confining—even claustrophobic for those who need, as I do at times, the panorama of plain or mountain. In the bush it is rare to be able to see 200 yards in any direction, and here a man cannot wander freely among far-spaced pines, as I have done in the West, by minding a mountaintop or two. There is no eyeballing your way through the bush. To travel even short distances here you need map and compass, the map to determine the bearing of your destination, and the compass to follow that bearing—laboriously, from tree to tree to tree—through the woods and swamps. There are certain pleasures in orienteering, but in my state of mind it is a tedious, even grim business, this lining up tree after tree with the wire-hair set into the slot of a compass lid.

My map of the immediate area is richly inlaid with contour

lines and other cartographic symbols, but today I know the map is a lie. Its land-parts should be white to symbolize the blank, the sea of trees to the north of me that is as trackless as any desert, wet or dry. Maybe for the cartographer in the airplane, the tooled and colored map that he has drawn from aerial photographs would make some sense. It would make none to me were I to strike out into the bush. Down on the earth, buried beneath the treetops like an ant crawling through spires of grass, I would find the land features recorded on the map as dubious as the angels that dance on the heads of pins. The contour lines are doubtful because the differences in elevation are so slight and so gradual, and the map doesn't work when you can't see the forest for the trees. One's position at any given moment is unknown—unknowable, given my crude instruments and even cruder human senses—and even one's destination, which is most often a section of squiggled line separating the blue and green, becomes after a while as suspect as the far side of the moon. Over the next rise? Over the tenth rise past the one just ahead? Is that a rise?

Despite such uncertainties, everything is familiar in the bush, each sponge of muskeg, each tangled clump of alder, each stand of pine or aspen or spruce, each deadfall. But when everything is familiar, nothing is; the trees and swamps and deadfalls seem merely to be illustrations of their kind, mirrors of each other. In the end, the contour lines, the line-tufts representing swamp, and all the other symbols mean nothing at all. It is the trees that count, the denseness of them, the sameness of them, the mindless malignant glut of them that stretches unbroken to the tundra in the far North. Each tree is like a wave, individual and distinguishable from the next, yet ephemeral, too, as the trekker makes his way through them, and each individual tree is soon lost in the sea of particularity. The trees become one, and each swamp, each hill is indistinguishable from the next. Between starting point and ending point there is only the blot of space, and there are no points of true reference except the mind that looks for them. When you have had too much of the me and not enough of the not-me, it is useless to run off into the bush because it is incomprehensibly vast, and the only thing you will find there is yourself.

Knowing these things, I almost climb back into the tree where the wind at least was sharp and new, but a tree is no place for a sound and sober man to spend the day. Tomorrow, if it comes to that, will be time enough to think of tree-sitting. For now, I know there is nothing, absolutely nothing left for me to do but to walk through the gray and windy gloom to the cabin and hunker down.

I do not go gently: but I go.

My reading of the weather that day turned out to be correct but, in a manner of speaking, premature—by some five or six hours. Late in the afternoon even a man whose senses were not so finely tuned as mine might have detected that the swells were subsiding, the brutal wind dying away. Before the sun set I saw the end of my confinement—I mean not the roadhead at the public landing but the westernmost edge of the low clouds. Their bellies were pebbled like cement and as black as thunderheads on the trailing edge, which was as straight and clean as if it had been trimmed with a mason's trowel. Behind the clouds was a widening band of blue so bright that it seemed to glitter up against the black, and, hanging in the west, shining like hot brass, was the found sun.

I could not sleep that night and for my troubles—or rather because of them—I got the gift of light. I keep my watch by night, too, and I know these shores almost as well by moon as by sun. Most nights the wind dies to nothingness in this country, and it is the quietest place on earth. There is magic in such nights and I go out to be hunted down by it, to be struck dumb. Sometimes after the moon rises above the trees I walk through its light down to the Wash Rock, which is clean and milky under the moon, and I sit next to the water, gathering up from the rock what heat is left in it from the day's sun. The silence has planed the water to a hard and perfect smoothness, and across the tiny bay is a line of shaggy cedars rimming the shore. Their trunks are tooled with moonlight and shine like pewter. The delicate bearberry and lithe slim sedge growing in the shallows are stiff and still, as if they have been cast in glass.

Nothing moves: no plant, no animal, not even my shadow on the dead rock. I listen: There is only the sound of myself, breath of my body's life, then not even that. This is the beginning of the world. In this time and place there is only rock, water, light, the irreducible inanimate earth from which all things flow. The force of such stillness drives deep into me: Something is going to happen. The silence is so fat I know that something must issue from it, and I wait for the birth. Holding my breath at water's edge, I can feel some essence or meaning or voice in the night air and in the very rock that holds me. It is traveling to me from everywhere at the speed of light, and with each passing second it is infinitely closer. I know that if I can wait only two seconds, one second more, I will hear some great thing. If I can only wait.

But I never can wait long enough for these last things, which would probably strike a man dead, and instead I fall prey to the cruel joys of first things. It is the fact-ness of the earth, the rough and smooth and the hard and soft and the light and dark of it, that draws me to the Wash Rock on such nights. I love that fact-ness, which is austere and wonderfully visible and unadorned on moonlit nights, yet at the same

131

time I fear that fact-ness—and there is some hate in this kind of fear—because the earth is mute. Underneath the surface things, or infused in them, I perceive a mystery, which I hope is a holy mystery, yet the closer it moves toward me, or I toward it, the farther away it is, and my passion on these nights is to hear and know this profound and unimaginable secret—no matter that it would strike me dead. But I cannot find out this last thing. Somehow, though, the love always overbalances the fear because the shining mystery I see on the surface vivifies and sweetens my own sense of and feeling for this strangeness called life. So I sit on the rock sweetly suffering in the moonlight and marvel at first things, which are themselves ever more profound and mysterious: that I am here, exactly here, in this time, in this place; that I am anywhere at all; that there is rock and water and light; that there is matter, something instead of nothing. But I am a small boy who has learned to read the words but not the meanings, and even though I study these first things, I cannot encompass or grasp even them. Again I have stepped to the outermost edge, and there is nothing to say or to think, and my mind is lost once more in the spectral silence.

Most of the time I am struck dumb with the gift of light, but sometimes, such as the night that ended my latest captivity here, it happens that instead of being driven away from speech, I am just as forcibly driven to it. Wide awake that night, I followed the beam of my flashlight through the moonless midnight to the Toe to check out the weather before trying to get some sleep. Even though there was no cloud cover to trap the earth's heat, the air was warm and strangely springlike. Through the ragged shifting canopy of trees I caught glimpses of dim stars as they glittered and then disappeared. A remnant of wind gentled the branches high above me, yet down on the path at a man's height all was still, and I could only hear the healing wind that was purling through the treetops—it was as if the sound were there to remind me of my smallness, or perhaps to prepare me for new and fantastic knowledge of it.

This is a place I know by now, yet even though the night sky had disappeared for four days, I was unmindful of the ways in which it could make itself new—but sometimes such lethargic blindness is to our good. Walking out onto the Toe, I switched off the light to look and listen, and as I surveyed the shore and sky and my eyes became acclimated to the blue-black night, I began to see colors under the starlight, the powder-green of the boat behind me, even the red in my flannel shirt. This was the sky of the strong woods, without even a farm light to mar it, infinitely deep, not the flat city sky with its stars pasted to it. To improve the reality of its four dimensions, I lay down on the Toe to blot out the earth. My feet pointed south, and as I stared into the depths above my brow, there they were:

At first they came slowly and secretly, and I wondered whether perhaps I was watching the great diagonal band of the Milky Way shifting—in my mind. It had been a day for that. Were they there? I squinted. My eye was as sharp as I could make it. But this was mystery: If I looked too directly I saw nothing. I looked away, waited, looked back, and then there was no doubt. Certainly I saw them. Northern lights! Northern lights! I watched as wedges of ashen light formed in the northern hemisphere. They were barely there but there just the same, two wedges of light, their substance and color as fragile as the finest blue ash of cold burnt wood. At first the lights grew slowly, almost timidly. Then the wedges became streams and the streams curtains that fell from some far place out past the strength of light. With increasing boldness they filled the northern quadrants, and the lights ceaselessly rose and fell, shifted from north to south and from east to west, up and down and across at every angle, and they died only to appear and reappear again and again. As if the universe were at play, the whole northern sky began to shimmer and dance in elegant ecstasy. The sky pulsed with worlds of energy, and like the French voyageurs who had seen the lights centuries before me, I heard music, or perhaps made my own, as each cadenza of light trilled from the sky. My jaw wide, I lay on the rock impaled by spears of light.

Then, as if I had not been dazzled enough, the lights began to show themselves in magnificently tender pastels, reds and yellows and purples and greens that fell for ages at unearthly speeds. As a drift of green shot down from directly above, I began to lose myself amongst the celestial lights. But then my ear snagged on a sound of the solid earth. I heard the lap and drip of an animal slaking its thirst. Zip was three feet away taking a drink, and I watched the lights and listened to the beads and streams of water falling like pebbles from her whiskered mouth. For a moment I lived in two worlds and I sang a song: "Ahh!" At first I was not even aware of what I had done, but it was one of the truest things I ever said. It was a prayer of praise and adoration, the song from a tick of dust, alive and singing what praise it could, hosannas to God, whoever He is, in the highest. In that moment I did not stop to ask whether my song was wanted. It was enough only to sing.

I catch my wonder—or it catches me—not so much in the workings of a bug or an atom as in spacious and powerful things like storm and light, and I must have lain on the Toe for almost two hours that night gazing up into the lights. Even though I had one of the best seats—or beds—in the house, it was not easy for me to lie passively on that rock. It is enough to sing—but it is enough only for a while. After the first euphoria had brought forth my plain song, I was seized by another euphoria, this one more studied but in its way just as strong, which demanded that I—or at least someone—*do something*. This needed to be shouted out, and I wanted to wake the world with a sound as glorious as these lights. I wanted Bach himself at the keyboard of a great organ I saw hung in the southern sky. Dwarfed as he was by the silvered and polished pipes reflecting the dance of lights, I could hear him spreading the news, the pipes blowing tunefully at full force in the controlled abandon of a Bach fugue. But the pipes blew only for me.

Bach was not there as he should have been, so it was left to me. I wanted my kind to add to the spectacle, to take part in it somehow, to broadcast it, and if that is still praise, it is praise mottled with thought. Less benignly, maybe I even wished to steal some of the far glory for myself. In between the showers of lambent light, I began to recall other nights these lights had added wonder to my world, and it was necessary to count the ways I had seen them: tonight, as a cadenza of colored lights; on a winter night when I lived on the edge of the northern plains, as a starburst that had quaked unseen out of a shattered core and then frozen in the crystalline cold; on another winter night, as a blossom, a blooming umbel of light; and last June, as blood made of light, the streams and trickles dripping into the black, scoring and staining the sky from the north all the way to the south rim.

But it was necessary not only to count the ways but to describe them, and I wanted pencil and paper, if not to write some music, which would have been the best thing to do, then at least to write some words. Without my tools I had to say the words aloud in hopes of remembering them, and though some of them are on these pages, most of them were lost. As the words rolled from my throat, I knew that this time the words were not for God but for myself and others.

The others? My only companion could not be interested in anything past her nose. The sky was out of her range and she was bored—in fact, she had gone for a swim. Man's best friend was dog-paddling around the Toe, and I had the heavens all to myself.

So it was that the wind and the night lights told me what I am. I have lived the summer alone and discovered myself— my self—to be a fit companion, but on that last day of my house-arrest two weeks ago, I fronted another fact that has been furtively lurking about for some time now: I am also a man amongst men, and that should not be—that cannot be— forgotten. The dog and myself were no longer companions enough. It is natural and health-giving to live alone, but it is not so if you are alone for too long.

Sometimes I want my life to be a changeless river that runs smooth and clear from birth to death, but I know that my life is not a river. It is more like this lake, and I need to watch my wave so that I can know when it will die, or if it is a different kind of wave that I am riding, when it will crest and crash.

It is hard to read these waves. During the last couple of weeks I have wondered whether perhaps there are not months of good riding left in this one. I've been to town since the blow and gotten a respite from myself, and September's transgressions against me—real or fancied—have all been forgiven. September may be the worst of the fair-weather months, but she makes up for it by being the best of them, too, and in these last days she has been at her best. I've been living bluebird days. Each day the lemon sun runs its course unobscured by a single cloud. A cool breeze blows across the land from out of the northwest, winnowing from the air what little dust accumulates there, and everything is sharp and clean. The sky is that rich blue I have seen only on mountaintops and here in the Quetico during the dying of summer. The sky seems no darker—at least to my eyes. Instead I would say that somehow there is more of it. The sky is hard-packed and gemlike, and if the blue were not without imperfections, it would seem that you could cleave it like a diamond. Because of the breeze it is cool, even chilly, on the water, and at night the temperature drops into the low forties or high thirties, and I pile blankets at the foot of the bed for those hours just before dawn when the tail end of the smoke thread has at last been drawn through the eye of the chimney and all the wood warmth is gone from the cabin. But during the day it is warm and still back in the woods, and the air is drowsy or brisk, as you like it: Take your pick. Sometimes I hunt out a likely clearing and lie down with a book or with only my thoughts and draw in the warmth. The brown brittle leaves rustle beneath me, and I shift my position to hear them crackle and to renew their warm redolence. They smell of smoke and old books, which in a way they are.

My sole complaint about this last week, if it is permissible to carp that the world lacks perfection, is that these September days are not long enough, but I suspect that I would be making the same complaint even if I could somehow extend the daylight by three hours back to the length of the summer solstice. Time slows here, but not really, and even though one day shades into the next and I can lose track of them and forget that they have names and numbers, the shortened daylight reminds me that the days pass just the same. Time is no longer the undercurrent of my days, as it has been for much of the summer. Again, it is the current.

Like the plant and animal world, I have been living fast—though not feverishly—to get in as much of this life as I can. With the passing of the August dog days, the fish are biting once more, and in the morning or evening I usually fish Nym's own Grand Bank, a strip of sandy shallows at the far east end of the lake. Nym is cooling quickly—I am reminded of that because the baths I take off the end of the Toe are again experiences that require more and more mental preparation as the days go by—so I know also that the lake trout will soon be rising to within reach of my (sometimes) regrettably unspecialized fishing tackle. Lake trout feed in water of forty-two degrees—or so at least everyone hereabouts seems to agree—and I have been trolling Nym's deepest trench with my largest plug and fattest sinker. I have great expectations, but so far I have managed to catch only the image of a stiff-tailed trout, which is invariably accompanied by another image—I have never learned to fish only for the sport of it—that of the trout's pink flensed flesh baking in my oven.

Having spent so many hours cabin-bound during the late windy and rainy weather, I'm even more glad for these bluebird days. Being as appreciative as I am, I've been trying to put such grand days to their best use, and I've been out and about every day this last week. A few days ago I packed a lunch and spent the day wandering the logging tote-roads above the low range of hills east of Nym. I'd been on the tote-road only once before, that time on a solo canoe trip I took in July to explore—or snoop around—Nickleby, Niobe, and Como Lakes, which lie immediately to the northeast of Nym.

It was, I hoped, a suitably foolish thing to decide to end my solo trip by portaging down the tote-road from Como back into Nym—a canoe trip is not much of a canoe trip unless the potential for some sort of disaster is built into it, and this had been a rather tame three days. As I tried to decide whether I should portage the tote-road, I knew there were several possibilities. The tote-road might not be there at all—not an uncommon occurrence—in which case I would have to retrace my route and return to Nym across the portage from Nickleby. If, in fact, the road were there, as the map claimed, it might be overgrown and untraceable for tens—

hundreds—of yards, or the road might simply peter out a half-mile into the bush. But more likely, the dotted line on the map that hooked down from Como and *almost* skirted Nym's east edge denoted the general principle of tote-roads, so to speak, and not the actual maze of them that was there. My task was made more difficult because I was alone and would have to portage almost 200 pounds of gear, which included my ancient and ailing wood and canvas Seliga canoe, as superb on the water as she is hopelessly heavy on portages. Carrying such tonnage, I would have to leap-frog my gear across the portage, and if I wasn't careful, I could have packs and canoe irretrievably strung out through the bush. I could, of course, have walked the tote-road first to see whether it actually did pass Nym's shore, but on long portages—this one would be a mile and a half or two—my interest tends to flag, and the excitement of uncertainty is the best antidote I know.

As it turned out my suspicions were correct. The single dotted line on the map was a symbol of a symbol, and I had to contend with unmarked nuances—loops and curves and dead ends. For once, though, I chose well—I took only three wrong turns—and, after stumbling through three swamps and reaching what I later discovered was the last unmarked fork in the trail, I took the one less traveled by, and, as in the poem, it made all the difference. The trail petered out. Using the canoe yoked to my aching shoulders as a kind of brush-breaker, I bulled my way through the brush and across deadfalls buried out of sight in waist-high grass, and then through the trees I saw it, the lake, more blue and more real than I ever imagined it could be. It was my oasis, and I had only to paddle home with a slight late afternoon breeze at my back.

Every trail and tote-road is incomplete—and I am, too—until I've walked the whole of it. Wanting to stretch my legs, but not overly to expend myself at it, I waited until this week to go back to the tote-road, knowing that now the swamps would be almost dry and that the trail would offer some easy walking. It was cool enough on the lake to wear gloves as I went over in the boat, but it was warm under the sun in the windbreak of the woods, exactly the fine fall walking weather I had hoped for. After tying the boat on the low sandy shore, I walked a quarter-mile into the woods and found the tote-road, then followed it back to Como first, walking up a few dead-end alleys as I did so just to see what there was to see (swamps). Then I retraced my steps back to Nym and followed the trail as it paralleled the south and southeast shores of Nym. Eventually it dribbled out in a forest of mere sticks—a clear-cutting some ten or fifteen years old. Past Como Lake I saw no man-tracks other than my own, though when the hunting seasons open, I expect the road will see some foot traffic as far south as Nym. Moose seem to be the road's primary users—though I saw none I did see plenty of their droppings—and on the alder-grown sections of the trail, their comings and goings have kept open one of the tracks on the tote-road.

Such changes in six weeks! Though the tamaracks' downy needles had not yet begun to turn—I've always thought those needles were too tender for this country, but mournful enough—the huge ferns were tawny brown and looked as if they had been dead for years. In spots the trail was lavished with wafers of gold, the dying leaves of birch and aspen that line sections of the road. The spent leaves reminded me of gold coins, and though I stopped to examine some samples from the coin of the realm, none of them, unfortunately, was precious enough to keep, there being too many of them. The moose maple leaves were rimmed in red, and even the Labrador tea was turning—I say *even* because I never knew before that this shrub's narrow leaves shade from a dark full green to a smoky copper. I picked some of the burnt leaves for tea to see whether the rusty death-fire would concentrate the brew made from them, but I found later that the fire had instead burnt away all the taste.

I stopped for lunch at a dilapidated log bridge that crossed the Nym River a half-mile or so east of the lake. The river runs, if that is the word, out of Nym Lake and eventually meanders its way south to Pickerel Lake where it joins other headwaters on their way to Rainy Lake and eventually Hudson's Bay. On a map it looks doubtful that this stream can be navigated all the way to Pickerel, even in high water, yet there obviously are—or at least were—those of a different opinion: Immediately on reaching the stream I saw the telltale sign of aluminum canoes, silver scrapings (fool's silver?) shining sharply on the dark rocks beneath the stream surface. (Did they make it to Pickerel?)

The bridge across the river, which at that point was about thirty feet wide, had weathered to a soft silver. Three giant pine trunks spanned the river, and even though the huge torsos had begun to falter in their task of supporting the log roadbed, which had been laid corduroy-fashion parallel to the stream, the great trunks still looked venerable enough to me to qualify as true giants in the earth. Sitting on the edge of the downstream giant with my boots dangling above the water, I lazily ate my bread and cheese and threw Zip a few token shares, which she shamelessly begged from me with her sad amber eyes and then greedily lapped up with her slab tongue. Behind me I could hear the quiet rush of water over rock from somewhere upstream, but at the bridge all was as slow and quiet and easy as could be, and I sat watching the current gently combing the bright slim grass that grew from the sandy stream-bottom. The water acted as a lens that seemed now to sharpen and brighten rather than to distort the image of each thing that lay beneath the surface, and as the brilliant green strands of grass slowly drifted and waved in the water their motion mesmerized me, and I could not help calling to mind the complete naturalness of this water plant's common name, which years ago someone had told me was angel's hair. It seemed hardly to be a metaphor at all.

Living such grand days as these, I found it hard to believe that there were ever any other kind. Mrs. Maki, who keeps our boat for us during the winters, told me a few weeks ago that Charlie Erickson is looking for a winter caretaker to tend his island outfitting post on the lake, and I was tempted to offer him my services.

Yet I was only tempted. Even though it seems natural— more natural now than ever—that I am living alone seldom seeing anyone, and even as fine and pleasant as these last days have been, I think it has come time to leave Nym. Except on those days when the weather transforms Nym into a sort of island jailhouse, I live quite easily—quite comfortably—with myself. Perhaps too easily.

One morning about three weeks ago as I was sitting at the window reading, I thought I heard the low guttural rumble of an outboard—and voices. Zip growled instantly and I, too, was suspicious, and my pulse began to pound. Who? I looked out the window but could see nothing, so I walked part way down the path. Men: They were in a strange boat, dark, almost black, and I could hear the powerful sputter of their motor as it idled. The strange boat looked huge near mine nestled against the Toe. Someone was getting out of the boat—to steal the motor? to tow my boat away? I walked a bit further down the path and stood on the hill among the trees where I knew they could see me. My eyes were cold, my blood hot, but all they could see was my stance. It was warning, ritual, ceremony: Know that someone is here, *know that someone is here, goddammit, and that I will fight for what is mine.*

But they were awesomely stupid and seemed unable—
unwilling?—to read my sign. One of the trespassers was
unloading things from the boat they had come in. *Unloading?*
Perplexed, I walked the rest of the way to the landing, being
sure not to hurry too fast, where the man stood with his back
to me near a pile of—what? There was a breeze out of the
west and he seemed not to have heard me as I came down
the path. Then the boat was leaving and two men in it waved
to me—to me? What was happening? I tried to take in
everything, and like a bird's my eyes darted about, trapped
in a mix of instants—shapes and colors and textures: the
man—his denim jacket and jeans; a backpack—gray—nylon?;
some wet cardboard—beer bottles in there silver—a wrench
gleaming in the grass; sun; the man's hat—denim too?—
shaped funny, like a fireman's; broken glass—brown—yes,
the beer bottles. Then the man turned to face me and I saw
dried mud caked on the welts of his boots. It was the wrong
color for this country. There was a rip in the knee of his jeans,
and a brassy button on the jacket shone in the sun. Then I
saw the blue eyes and the full strawberry-blond beard. It was
Rick—Rick!

There was a hand outstretched, and then I remembered
and fumbled for the hand and shook it. I looked at Rick's face
and behind the lush beard it was red and grinning—grinning
at what?—and he was saying something. He asked me a
question but I forgot to answer, and he asked me again. I was
still pumping his arm. "Oh! How am I?" I repeated after him.
I searched for the right words but I could only say, "Fine.
Fine. Fine."

It was surprising—disturbing—to find out how easily and
thoroughly I could become disoriented. As innocuous as this
"intrusion" was, it was still too much for me, and my mind
was surfeited and numbed by all that was new. Even now
after Rick has come and gone, I can't make of those bits and

pieces a whole experience, and his arrival lies shattered in my mind like the beer bottle on the rock. What I remember about Rick's arrival is the sense of paralysis—and the panic—that stemmed from my inability to collate the odds and ends into one piece. My mind had simply gone blank from the false surfeit, and at first I wanted to attribute the disjointedness to the sheer surprise of Rick's arrival—he had come a day earlier than I had expected and he'd been lucky enough to find a ride out to the cabin with a couple of college kids working for Charlie Erickson.

But the surprise wasn't the thing. Since then, before going to town each week I have tried to prepare myself for meeting people, but I do not know how to make such preparations—or even whether they can be made. I find myself increasingly unable to judge how much of myself, as it were, to give to people. Last week—and it is somewhat of an embarrassment to discover these things later—I tried to buttonhole the woman in the post office who gives me my mail, but she was obviously too busy to be buttonholed—there were two people waiting in line behind me. Yet, to the bartender in the basement of the Steep Rock Hotel, who tried for some small talk with me an hour later on that sleepy September afternoon, I had nothing to say. I picked up my beer and sat at a table to escape his friendliness. The transition that I must make between living with myself and interacting with others, between this world—how small!—and the world past these shores, is becoming increasingly difficult. I am, simply, losing my capacity, though not my desire, for others.

At Nym I have only to relate to myself, and though it has not always been easy or pleasant to do that, it has been simpler. The solitude has allowed me to live my life stripped of the usual confusions and irrelevancies that scatter one's force and cloud perception. There are times when I need nothing so much as the psychological simplicity of solitude, and to live alone is a skill that I have come to regard as much worth cultivating, but at the same time it also seems true that solitude is one simplicity I cannot afford for too long.

As I have said, there are signs that my solitude is now exacting too much from me, that it is pointing me toward the hermetic life, which by definition—at least by my definition—is a form of madness. I have decided, though, that there was no touch of madness in my sitting high in a pine on a windy afternoon mouthing blasphemies to the wind. If there has been any craziness in the past weeks, I think it much more likely that I succumbed, not in the pine tree or on the Wash Rock in the moonlight or on the Toe in the midst of the northern lights, but on the sunny Nym River that day I gazed so tranquilly into the stream. I was more than mesmerized by the angel's hair wafting in the water: I was transfixed by it, and somehow the implication of that moment was that angel's hair is enough—or at least that it ought to be enough. The longer I live apart from people, the more easily I am seduced into believing such lies, and I seem to believe them for longer periods of time. Perhaps angel's hair and all that it represents ought to be enough, but in my clearer states of mind—for instance, when I am sitting in treetops or basking under the northern lights—the very idea strikes me as unmindful, almost disrespectful, of the given: Angel's hair can never be enough.

Angel's hair is necessary to my life, but—to borrow a useful distinction from the logicians—it is not sufficient. I require something else in addition to the natural world; I require, not the mere aggregate of society—the hive—but something rarer and more difficult to achieve, namely, community. Men live in society because society holds out the hope for community: It is in community that men *live*. Not, of course, that we live only there. If I have discovered anything this summer, it is that solitude in its own way is as life-giving as society, and I know that if I were denied the one, the other would not be diminished in my eyes: It would be worthless. So, I am sanest when I live in two worlds, when I am swept away by veils of light and at the same time caught on the sounds of my dumb drinking dog, who reminds me of where I am and of what I am.

What am I? To remind myself: I am a social creature striving to surmount the aggregate of the hive so that I might achieve community with my kind; I am a man striving to be a *Mensch*. Before leaving Salt Lake City last spring I promised myself that I would more diligently keep my journal so that I might have as complete a record as possible of this experiment. I wrote every day this summer and some days I wrote for hours, but the words were like the trees that fall in the forest where there is no one to hear them, and for the first time my journal began to presuppose a reader other than myself. I was making the discovery that, though it was easy to give up society, it was not easy to give up community—and that I had no intentions of giving it up. My occupation this summer, at times my preoccupation, has been to share my world, my sights and discoveries and musings, to share— paradoxically—my solitude. I was trying for two worlds. This book, which began as a journal, is a reaching out to my kind. It is my admission of the necessity for communion, and, in a sense somewhat different from what we usually mean by the phrase, these essays are labors of love.

Besides being labors of love, these essays are also what I won in the bet with myself. I was right: There is something at Nym worth seeing, worth discovering. There is, for one thing, the natural world, the world of rock and water and light, muscle and bone. Here I stretched my body, and because I ceased abusing it with the excesses of the city, I am again in its good graces (and wondering whether I can maintain that state of grace once I return to the city). But mostly what was here to discover or, more accurately, to carve or sculpt—was a set of opinions and beliefs. I did not find them, I formed them, as if their materials were wet clay and I were a craftsman adding clay here, subtracting it there so that I might get the figure right, which is to say to get it true, true as seen by the angle of my eye in this time and in this place. When I examine my self now I see a figure more distinctly outlined than the one I saw last spring. It is true that I might have carved out beliefs on other matters—and I almost did. To be sure, these beliefs amount to no *Weltanschauung*—I would need another twenty-eight years of life to presume to such a grand codification as that. So, not a world-view—but still, a view.

Though it satisfied me the summer, the writing is no longer enough, and this wave threatens to overbalance and fall. It is time to leave this cabin. Having shown signs that I am losing my capacity, if not yet my will, for flesh-and-blood human contact, I wonder whether it is but one more step to losing my will for that contact. Made up of mind, I need the dialogue that we trade from heart to heart and from mind to mind, whether in conversation or, as with me this summer, on a written page, and being made up of matter, too, I need simply to be with people again to be as fully human as I can.

I want to see my kind and feel the ambience of their presence, to again use my voice and hear their voices. And I want now to hear the voice of my still-estranged wife Suzanne. Love being a high form of belief, I know that, like these words, it too can be—must be—crafted, and I am ready to test our voices in recrafting with her the solid communion we once shared.

In two days I will hear other voices again: Rick will be back then, and we have planned a five-day canoe trip into the

Quetico—may this weather hold—before I return to Salt Lake City. According to the calendar this is not strictly correct, but tomorrow is the last day of summer.

Everything is packed or put away. This morning I carried the washtub and scrub board up from the Wash Rock and stored them in the pantry along with the life jackets and my fishing gear. The five-gallon gas cans that sat in the clearing behind the Toe all summer are now next to the outhouse, ready to be stored there for the winter. A couple of cords of wood—I was a little over-zealous—are stacked neatly under the wide eaves and covered with plastic. I hope Bob and Rick have as much fun burning the wood this winter as I did cutting it. But I didn't steal all the fun for myself—I left another cord or so of eight-foot lengths piled in the woods that they can saw and split themselves. The cabin is swept— even dusted—but I never did get around to washing the windows, even though my resident orb-weaver left me weeks ago without sending a replacement. The bedding has been washed and aired, the clothesline is down and hangs in a shank from a nail in the pantry, and the evaporation cooler is stored in the loft. And I'm squeaky-clean—in honor of Rick's arrival today. In my closing up for the summer, my bath this morning was the one activity about which I wasn't strongly ambivalent. I'll be glad enough for a hot shower. All that remains now is to haul the shutters out from beneath the cabin and rehang them, but Rick and I will save that chore until after our canoe trip. After the padlock is once again on the door, we'll pull them out and hang them just before we walk down the path to the Toe for the last time.

On his postcard Rick says that since he's not sure what time he'll be leaving the farm this morning, he'll try to thumb a ride out to the cabin to spare either of us a long wait at the landing. But it's after Labor Day and he knows that he'll be lucky even to see a boat. If he's not at the cabin by 1:30 this afternoon, I'm to pick him up at the landing at 2.00.

Meanwhile, there isn't much left to do but to sit here at the table and wait for him. I'd hoped that I would be waiting for Bob, too, but he writes that he can't make it for this trip. He'll regret it—incredibly enough, these bluebird days still hold. Or rather, they've begun again. Yesterday morning I woke to see the ground pebbled with freak snow, but it all melted by midmorning.

I find myself wishing—but it's only a half-wish—that we'd planned this canoe trip for a week from now. I'll love Rick for walking up that path, but I'll hate him a little for it, too. Fortunately it's the kind of hate he could understand. I keep thinking of our meeting in late August, and I'm anxious for— and about—his coming. We'll spend the afternoon packing for the trip and poring over maps trying to decide where in the Quetico we want to go. Maps are appetizers with us— they set off a train of imaginings and sharpen our anticipations. Maybe we'll even get a little greedy and plan a trip that will have to be shortened in mid-route. Or maybe we'll plan not to have a plan and simply paddle off to see where we go. Whatever we decide, there will have to be compromises and concessions, not only in the planning but from here on out. Those are social graces I haven't exercised much this summer, and I find it ironic, but at the same time appropriate, that mine will first be tested not in the hive of some city but in a community of two on lakes more remote than Nym. I wonder how I'll do. The clock says high noon—I'll know in two hours.

—Voices! I'll know in minutes—no, seconds. Am I ready for this? I am. There stands Rick down in the clearing now: